PASSING THE

21 TESTS

OF

LEADERSHIP

Books by Larry Kreider

The Cry for Spiritual Mothers and Fathers

Your Personal House of Prayer

Hearing God 30 Different Ways

House To House

Biblical Foundation Series (12 Book Series)

Biblical Role of Elders for Today's Church

Growing the Fruit of the Spirit

Helping You Build Cell Churches

Starting a House Church

Supernatural Living

The 3 Loves

Passing the 21 Tests of Leadership

The Invitation: Church Planting Stories

What Every Small Group Leader Should Know

PASSING THE
21 TESTS
OF
LEADERSHIP

BIBLICAL INSIGHTS FOR LEAVING
A LEGACY OF LEADERSHIP & INFLUENCE

LARRY KREIDER

DESTINY IMAGE® PUBLISHERS, INC.
P.O. Box 310, Shippensburg, PA 17257-0310
"Promoting Inspired Lives."

Cover design by Eileen Rockwell

This book and all other Destiny Image and Destiny Image Fiction books are available at Christian bookstores and distributors worldwide.

For more information on foreign distributors, call 717-532-3040.
Or reach us on the Internet: www.destinyimage.com.

ISBN 13: 978-0-7684-1952-8
Ebook: 978-0-7684-1953-5
LP ISBN: 978-0-7684-1954-2
HC ISBN: 978-0-7684-1955-9

For Worldwide Distribution, Printed in the U.S.A.

1 2 3 4 5 6 7 8 9 10 11 / 22 21 20 19 18

Previously published as *21 Tests of Effective Leadership*; ISBN: 978-07684-3058-5

Dedication

This book is dedicated to our Lord Jesus Christ and to the many leaders I have been privileged to work with, and alongside, during more than 40 years of leadership and ministry.

Acknowledgments

Special thanks to Karen Ruiz, my writing assistant who does a superb job, and also my heartfelt gratitude to those who have taken the time to give input to this book: Katrina Brechbill, Peter Bunton, Deryl Hurst, Ron Myer, Steve Prokopchak, Brian Sauder, Sarah Sauder, and many others who allowed me to use their stories.

And a special thanks to the entire Destiny Image team. You have been wonderful to work with.

Endorsements

It is wonderful to be able to endorse this book *Passing the 21 Tests of Leadership*. In a day where so many excuses are made for people who fail in qualification, we now have a trustworthy presentation of the standards we should establish for leaders. Bravo, Larry, for another important contribution.

DANIEL JUSTER Th.D.
Director Tikkun International
Author of *Due Process* and other books.

In all arenas of life, we see a trend of failing leadership. This book by Larry Kreider is timely and an excellent tool to help correct this trend. These 21 tests must be passed if one is to be an effective leader, especially in God's Kingdom. Larry writes from life experience, and his journey will inspire you to press on through challenges and see them as tests, knowing that they will equip you to become a leader who truly represents the King. Thanks, Larry, for sharing your life; you live what you have written.

TONY FITZGERALD
Apostolic Leader of Church of the Nations

With *Passing the 21 Tests of Leadership* Larry has again compiled another practical volume of vignettes, anecdotes, and principles for leaders in the Church and the marketplace. Consistently, he encourages us to see every day challenges of life and leadership from the perspective of overcomers, not victims.

The discussion questions provide a valuable way to personalize choices at both crossroads and in crises. I envision seasoned and emerging leaders sitting together to profitably explore the applications of these tests.

KEITH YODER

Founder and President, Teaching the Word Ministries

Author of *Healthy Leaders, Pennsylvania*

Larry Kreider is a leader of leaders, and one who has my utmost respect, trust, and friendship. I encourage every believer who desires to reach his or her maximum leadership potential to invest in this book, and glean from the seasoned insight of one of the Body's true Apostolic leaders.

ROBERT STEARNS

Eagles' Wings Ministries, New York

Contents

Introduction

Every person with the potential for leadership—and that is everyone—will face a series of tests. None are exempt. I know. I have faced test after test after test in life during the past 40 plus years in both the business world and in the Church world. And it did not stop there. My marriage has been tested, my family has been tested, relationships have been tested, my security has been tested, my reputation has been tested, and our finances have been tested. In fact, I have faced so many tests that a few years ago I started to compile them into a list, and as a result you have this book of 21 tests in your hands! But before I go on, allow me to give you some good news up front. God does not set up this "leadership training course" for us to fail! You will, however, continue to face the same tests again and again and again until you pass them.

Life is filled with all kinds of tests: Driver's tests, pop quizzes, exams, and midterm tests in school. We get our blood pressure tested and our eyes tested. Every product we purchase has been thoroughly tested to be sure it will stand up under pressure.

I am writing the introduction to this book from the seat of United Airlines flight 681, flying to the West Coast of the United States of America. I am certainly relieved this airplane has gone through a safety test before it took off from the Chicago airport a few hours ago. Imagine boarding a plane that has not been tested for safety. It would be ludicrous to trust such a plane. In the airline industry everything is methodically tested. The pilots have been tested during years of prior training. The flight attendants were also trained and tested. Even every passenger was examined (tested) before boarding this plane to be sure they did not bring a weapon on board.

All of us will be tested so we can stand in the heat of the battles we will face. The greater our call to leadership, the greater the tests we will face. The Bible is filled with examples of those who were tested and then went on to become phenomenal leaders—some leading God's people and others providing leadership to whole nations. From Daniel to Joseph to Moses to Deborah to Jesus, we see those who led with endurance and strength, but they all faced great tests.

In the Bible we read,

> *When troubles come your way, consider it an opportunity for great joy. For you know that when your faith is tested, your endurance has a chance to grow. So let it grow, for when your endurance is fully developed, you will be perfect and complete, needing nothing* (James 1:2-4).

There is a great need for leaders today who have been willing to be examined by the tests of life so they will endure during difficult times. Our God allows tests in our lives to prepare us for our future roles of leadership. If we lack anything today in the world we live in, it is secure, mature, and consistent leaders who have been willing to be tested. We don't need more positions filled. We need leaders in all walks of life who will lead in humility and strength. This type of leader can only be developed by embracing, enduring, and passing the tests they will face.

My life has been a series of tests. I have faced the test of insecurity many times. I have been tested with the test of perseverance so many times I have lost count. I just wanted to quit innumerable times! I have experienced the tests of my calling, the humility test, the teamwork test, the releasing test, the priorities test, the transition test, the criticism test, the conflict test, the test of unmet expectations, the test of timing…the list goes on and on.

So then, I invite you to join me on my journey as I open my life to you and share with you 21 tests that I have faced personally. I added dozens of stories of others who have faced these same tests and how they eventually passed. My guess is that you will also need to embrace these same tests as God prepares you for your present and future role of leadership. It really helps to know what the tests may look like before we take them so we can be prepared for them when they come.

And for the record's sake, I am still facing these and other tests so I can be the leader God has called me to be. This list of 21 tests is by no means exhaustive. But I can promise you that if you will embrace these 21 tests and allow the Lord to develop your attitude, your character, and your abilities, you will be prepared for the leadership He has for you. Let's get started.

LARRY KREIDER

Chapter 1

The Calling Test

An effective leader will discover his calling and
trust God to manifest it.

It's a typical June afternoon at Jefferson High School. The crowded hallways are hectic and loud as the kids jostle for position in the already stifling hot building.

Owen Taylor, the principal at Jefferson, stands in the hallway watching the living, breathing, seething wave of humanity. It's hard to believe, but it's been seven years since he took the helm of this dilapidated building splattered with graffiti and with students from some of the most troubled neighborhoods in the city.

Reminiscing, Owen remembered that for the first couple of years he felt as though he was banging his head against a wall. Not only was there a shortage of space for the students in the classrooms, but their textbooks were torn and tattered and usually more than ten years old. As if that were not enough, he had the challenge to reduce the high rate of school drop-outs—not the students, but the teachers. Teaching these kids was more than most teachers bargained for. Breaking up frequent fights, coupled with the challenge of absenteeism and low test scores had teachers running for the door after a short time of teaching at Jefferson.

Owen's idealism, when he first came to lead Jefferson, was quickly tempered by a strong dose of reality. It was a far more demanding job than he ever could have prepared for, but he persevered. He hoped to change the environment, and, as a Christian, he knew it was an opportunity to serve a school that desperately needed help.

He rallied his staff, sharing with them a vision of what Jefferson could be. Although he faced a myriad of challenges as he attempted to lead his school down the path to academic excellence, Jefferson's proficiency rate in reading and math assessments gradually increased. The raise in test scores did not go unnoticed. It got Jefferson off Pennsylvania's warning list of schools facing the state's intervention due to poor standards and earned the school bonus money as a reward.

Owen's track record of success captured the attention of other schools. Unexpectedly, one day a successful school with state-of-the art facilities offered Owen a job with an incredible salary increase. Owen and his wife had just bought a home. A salary increase would make life so much easier. He felt guilty for even considering it. But a more financially stable school would have fewer hurdles to cross. *I'm really not being paid enough for what I do here,* Owen thought. *I'm overworked. I have to think of my family. I'll never get another chance like this.*

The new job offer was tempting. Owen anguished, *God, what do you want me to do? Am I really called to help combat the challenges of poverty and the poor educational achievement in a low-income school district? I could just as well help teachers and students in a better school who actually want to excel and be in the classroom! Am I truly called to lead at Jefferson? I want to be in the center of Your will for my life. What do you want me to do?*

Owen was facing the test of his calling.

—⁂—

Like Owen, your God-given calling is likely to be tested. Yours may be a leadership call in business, education, government, community service, the Church, your family, your neighborhood, the arts, entertainment, media, or sports. No matter what your vocation, it is inevitable that there will come a time when you begin to doubt yourself and what God has called you to do. You will wonder if your work really is God-ordained or important in His Kingdom. If you are like me, you have gone through times of doubt as you struggled to find a sense of purpose in your life's work. You may begin to doubt if you have a calling at all. Don't despair! Rest assured that God is in the business of equipping and calling leaders. God will not call you to something He does not give you the grace to do.

God Gives You Talents and Gifts

If you are unsure what your call is right now, know that God has given you *talents* and *gifts* to help you figure out your *calling*. Aristotle said that "Where your talents and the needs of the world cross, lies your calling."[1] But it is rarely that easy. Although you should use your talents and gifts to serve others, a calling is so much more.

First of all, let's look at your *talents*. Your talents are those things God has deposited within you to excel, such as the following: public speaking, teaching, singing, mathematics, debate, accounting, writing, painting, cooking, interior design, working with children, sales, and many others. Your talents make certain types of work attractive to you. And because they represent natural skills you already have or can easily develop, you excel when you use them.

When David was anointed as the next king, you would have expected him to enter the royal court in some managerial or top-level capacity. But he did not. He gained entrance as a lowly harpist. God used his harp-playing skills to get him noticed in the king's court. In the same way, you can look at your flair for public speaking or preaching, your love of writing, or your ability to work with figures and be assured that God can use and develop your talents which will eventually prepare you for your calling.

In addition to your talents, you also have God-given *gifts!* Your gifts are spiritual areas of life that God has blessed you with. "In his grace, God has given us different gifts for doing certain things well..."[2] Your gifts may include teaching, service, preaching, encouragement, generosity, music, hospitality, and so on. No matter what the gift is, God is the source of the gift, and it equips you to fulfill His call. God has uniquely gifted you. Your call will take advantage of your strengths—those qualities and abilities He's given you. He wants you to do great things—for His purpose, His Kingdom, and His pleasure. Since He is the Giver of all gifts, your success completely depends on His activity through you and your dependence upon Him.

How to Discover Your Calling

Just using your talents and gifts, however, does not mean you have been *called* by God. Your call is so much more than doing something you are good at.

How can you discover your calling? Your calling comes as a significant impression from God. You realize this call is the Holy Spirit working within you. It's a conviction about what you are to do with your life at this particular time. It is something that feeds your passion. It is that unexplained, God-given desire deep in your soul that excites you whenever you think about it. Finding that "sweet spot" where your abilities and interests align with God's purposes and intersect with the world's needs is something many leaders long to achieve. Your calling is something you do because it gives you a sense of fulfillment of God's plan for your life.

> **Your calling is that unexplained, God-given desire deep in your soul that excites you whenever you think about it.**

Most leaders know their calling involves more than one passion and more than one talent. One of my vocations is to write books. I am currently writing this book from Nairobi, Kenya. I took a break today between leadership meetings where I was serving as a consultant and a mentor, in order to write. And tomorrow I look forward to writing on my long plane trip home as I travel from Zurich, Switzerland, to Washington-Dulles Airport. I love to write! It is a passion of mine. It is that personal "sweet spot" for me.

Eric Liddle was a Scottish runner who competed in the 1924 Olympics. He had a calling as a missionary, but he also had a calling to run. When he was challenged by his sister to go immediately to serve as a missionary in China rather than competing in the Paris Olympics, Eric acknowledged that God made him for a purpose—to be a missionary, "...but he has made me fast, and when I run, I feel God's pleasure."[3] He knew that for this particular point in time, God had called him to run competitively.

God knows that if we are passionate and fulfilled in what we do, we will be cheerfully and unselfishly occupied in our work as co-laborers with Christ. The apostle Paul is an example of someone who discovered his God-given calling after using his talents in a very destructive manner. In the Book of Acts, Paul (then called Saul), was using his zeal, passion, and gift of teaching to persuade people not to follow God. In fact, he persecuted and imprisoned those who believed in Christ. But after he met Christ in a personal way and was filled with the Holy Spirit, Paul used those same gifts to help lead many people to Christ. In addition to using his natural talents and spiritual gifts, he had discovered his life's calling.

God has a great redemptive plan for our lives. For example, an unscrupulous money manager who has swindled thousands of dollars from clients, when he is redeemed, will use his talent for allocating capital for clients in productive ways—helping rather than hurting them.

Know That You Are Called

God's call comes to people in different ways. Biblical accounts of God's call vary greatly. It would be so much easier if God called us all in the same predictable way. Instead, He expects us to be sensitive and obedient to His direction as He leads step by step.

Sometimes fellow Christians have an important role in confirming or correcting your perception of God's call. Because everyone will not understand your response to God's call, you should prayerfully listen to fellow believers who encourage or question your pursuit of a particular calling. God may be speaking through them.

The Bible records that most leaders were not seeking a position of leadership when God intervened in their lives and called them. Some leaders that God called did not think they could lead (Moses). Some leaders felt that other people would be better leaders. Yet if God calls us, whoever we are, we should be ready and willing to accept that call. In fact my personal observation is that God is glorified in using people whom the world perceives as weak or unlikely leaders. Take Peter, for example. In modern terms, he was a blue collar worker, an uneducated fisherman. He was not religious or part of the priesthood, and moreover, he often put his foot in his mouth and jumped to conclusions. Yet God used him in a major way!

As a leader, you must know you are called. Then you can say, along with Paul, the apostle, that you are *"chosen by the will of God..."* (1 Cor. 1:1) and *"not appointed by any group of people or any human authority, but by Jesus Christ Himself..."* (Gal. 1:1). For example, if you are a pastor, you have heard God's call and have an inner conviction and desire to lead the family of God in your local church. This desire requires a passion and calling from God or you will want to give up when the task becomes difficult and demanding.

Seventeen years ago, I almost quit as the senior pastor of our church. My immaturity as a leader and my inability to communicate clearly the things that I felt God was showing me led to my frustration. After serving as a senior pastor for twelve years, I was ready to "throw in the towel." I felt misunderstood, and I was not sure if it was worth all the hassle. I was frustrated, exhausted, and overworked. In a misguided attempt to try to please everyone, I was listening to dozens of voices that seemed to be giving conflicting advice and direction. I felt unable to get back on track. I was tired and was encouraged to take a sabbatical. It was during the sabbatical, spending time with God in the mountains, that I remembered the original call from God to lead this church. And the call had not changed! God never told me to quit! I went back to my original call from God and led our church through a transition to decentralize into eight churches and then start a family of churches scattered all over the world. Today, by the grace of God, I am extremely fulfilled in my call and role of leadership.

Be Secure in Your Calling

Paul knew he was called by God to be an apostle and that is why he did not seek to win the approval of men. *"Obviously, I'm not trying to win the approval of people, but of God. If pleasing people were my goal, I would not be Christ's servant"* (Gal. 1:10). He was secure in his calling and encouraged others to know their individual calling as they lived a life of purpose and destiny. *"...Be sure to carry out the ministry the Lord gave you"* (Col. 4:17).

You must know that you are called by God to serve in a role of leadership. Otherwise, when the going gets tough, you will probably doubt yourself and question your decisions. Bear in mind, if someone talked you into a position of leadership, someone else can talk you out of it.

Like Paul, you must not only know you are called, you must be secure in the fact that you are loved and called by God to carry out the job He's given you to do. Discovering who you are means you let go of the person that you, or others, think you are, and instead you strive to be who Jesus wants you to be.

Your Calling May Change

As you enter different stages in your life, your calling may change. Sometimes your primary calling in life changes due to the fact that your priorities have changed. Your primary career may no longer fit your needs—perhaps because you are taking care of aging parents. Other times your business has changed and a downturn in the market outlook alters your field and revenue no longer meets your needs. Sometimes in midlife you discover a field of work that you feel called to that is totally different from what you are currently doing. You decide that any sacrifices you have to make to change your career will be worth the effort because you feel that God is calling you to change. My friend Deryl started a realty company and was a partner in this business for many years. But he changed his career in mid-life to pursue his passion for pastoral ministry. He is now an associate pastor in my local church.

Nowhere Else to Go But Into God's Calling

Paul also knew there was a cost to his calling because Christ said, *"Come after me, take up your cross, and follow me"* (see Matt. 16:24). Though tremendously fulfilling, any leadership role can be marked with pain, sacrifice, and conflict. Sometimes well-meaning people will say things that will test your call to your area of leadership. There will be those who disagree with your style of leadership. Some will think you make decisions too fast, and some will think you make decisions too slow. Others may question whether you should even be the leader. It is during times like these that you must know that God has called you.

In John 6, Jesus spoke a message that was too tough to swallow for many who were following Him. In fact, it caused many to desert Him. He declared that He was the living Bread and anyone who ate this Bread would live forever. Many could not understand what He meant. After many disciples subsequently left Him, Jesus turned to the Twelve and asked if they wanted to leave too.

Peter gives his famous response, *"Lord, to whom would we go? You have the words that give eternal life…"* (John 6:68). Peter knew that he was *called* to follow Jesus.

As a leader, you must know *where the Lord has called you* and *to whom you are called*. Peter had settled in his mind that he was called to Christ. There was nowhere else to go. It didn't matter if his fishing business was more profitable and could supply a better living for him. What mattered was that he was called to follow Jesus, and because he was called, he was not going anywhere or doing anything outside that call! You must be settled about where you are called to leadership for this season of your life and refuse to compromise, even when you are tested.

As a leader, you must know *where the Lord has called you* and *to whom you are called.*

Daniel, Joseph, and Esther are a few of the many biblical examples of godly people who were severely tested in their callings. Each of them was placed in situations where things seemed out of their own personal control, but they surrendered to God for them to achieve this end. They knew they were called for *"such a time as this"* (Esther 4:14). They persevered during the tests. Leaders grow when they are in situations that are out of their control. In these situations they have to depend totally on the Lord or they will fail.

Leaders that have been tested in their calling become secure and mature. When you serve the Lord with the ability and calling He has given you, you bring glory to His name and blessing to His people.

Now, back to Owen.

—ɯ—

Although a significant financial incentive was tempting, Principal Owen Taylor knew that his dilemma to stay or move on to another job came down to the question of knowing where he was called. He realized that to help a school like Jefferson High School was a special calling from God that gripped his heart. Staying at Jefferson, he could touch the lives of kids and teachers that would multiply in hundreds of ways and change the future lives of many families forever. He had always encouraged his teachers and students to start something and stick with it to the finish. Even though the new job offer was extremely tempting, he could not abandon his school. His calling was sure. He would no longer doubt his calling and leadership as a principal in the inner city. He would leave the details to God. How it all worked out was in the Lord's hands. He passed the calling test.

Endnotes

1.   Aristotle, 384-322 B.C., Quotation Gallery, http://malouescasa.i .ph/blogs/yousaidwhat/?p=245, Accessed July 29, 2009.

2.   Romans 12:6. See also First Corinthians 12.

3.   Eric Liddell, "Chariots of Fire," Internet Movie Database, Accessed August 6, 2009 from http://www.imdb.com/title/tt0082158/ quotes.

The Calling Test

Personal reflection questions/discussion

1. Describe your personal God-given calling.

2. Define the difference between talents and gifts.

3. Take the time to create a list of your natural and physical talents.

4. Now take the time to list your God-given gifts.

5. How do the two intersect in such a way that they fulfill or could fulfill a life call? Who will you serve with these gifts?

—ɯ—

Chapter 2

The Humility Test

Effective leaders give credit to others.

Anthony is a youth pastor of a large church. He loves people and investing his life in them. Most days you can find him spending time with the youth, even outside the regularly scheduled meetings and events. His office and his home is a magnet for kids to hang out and talk. They feel secure with Anthony because he loves them, accepts them for who they are, and cares for them. He has the gifts and grace to connect with teens in their world.

Yet as a leader, Anthony knows his limitations. Although he has great rapport with the kids, he is not a teacher. At youth meetings and events, he usually delegates the teaching role to Justin, a member of his staff. Justin is gifted as a teacher. Youth rallies and events are energized by his humor and gift of teaching as he deftly demonstrates how to integrate life and faith.

Recently, a region-wide youth event planned by Anthony and Justin was a phenomenal success. It thrust their church into the limelight, and since Justin was the speaker at most of the events, he was hailed and heralded, and received most of the credit for what happened there. One Sunday morning after the conference, Anthony listened in disbelief as Justin described the conference as his own innovative idea, basically claiming all the credit for its success as his own.

Anthony knew better. He knew he was the one who had put most of the hard work into planning and shaping the conference in every aspect— except the teaching. Yes, Justin did contribute heavily to the success with his charisma and wit in his teaching, but it seemed to Anthony that Justin had become a "legend in his own mind" and Anthony didn't like it! *I should just knock him down a peg or two*, Anthony fumed to himself. *I could easily hail my own accomplishments and set the record straight!* This was a humbling experience and a test of his humility as a leader. Would he pass the test?

—⁂—

Sometimes, you may be tempted to feel like Anthony when it seems obvious you should give a word of correction to someone because they have overstepped their boundaries. But as a leader, you must realize that your role is not just to accomplish a task. There is a process and attitude by which the job should be done. You must pray, not only for God to show you what to do and help you to get it done, but also that God would give you a proper heart-attitude. When you begin to get frustrated because someone just isn't "getting it," that's a signal that you need to confess to God a wrong heart and ask Him for His heart of compassion and humility.

What's Your Test Score?

There's an online test you can take for humility. Have you ever heard of it? It starts with these questions, "Do you flaunt your accomplishments? Love the sound of your own voice? Do you top your own list of 'Favorite People'? Find out how modest you are with The Humility Test!"

I don't know how accurate the online test is, but the biblical test is foolproof. It is found in First Peter 5:5, *"...clothe yourselves with humility toward one another, because, 'God opposes the proud but gives grace to the humble'"* (NIV). The word *clothe* in Greek means "to attach a piece of clothing to oneself." In the New Testament times, slaves attached a white piece of cloth on their clothing so that others would know that they were slaves. Peter exhorts us to tie the cloth of humility on ourselves in order to be identified as believers in Christ as we act humbly toward others. In this way, we will receive God's grace and help.[1]

A.W. Tozer once wrote an article called "Humility: True and False" and concluded:

> I have met two classes of Christians: the proud who imagine they are humble, and the humble who are afraid they are proud. There should be another class: the self-forgetful who leave the whole thing in the hands of Christ, and refuse to waste any time trying to make themselves good. They will reach the goal far ahead of the rest.[2]

In 1878, when William Booth's Salvation Army was beginning to make its mark, men and women from all over the world began to enlist. One man, who had once dreamed of becoming a bishop, crossed the Atlantic from America to England to enlist. Samuel Brengle left a fine pastorate to join Booth's Army. But at first General Booth accepted his services reluctantly and grudgingly. Booth said to Brengle, "You've been your own boss too long." And in order to instill humility in Brengle, he set him to work cleaning the boots of other trainees. Discouraged, Brengle said to himself, "Have I followed my own fancy across the Atlantic in order to black boots?" And then, as in a vision, he saw Jesus bending over the feet of rough, unlettered fishermen. "Lord," he whispered, "you washed their feet; I will black their shoes."[3]

Tests of Leadership

Our competitive culture encourages us to maneuver our way to the top and manipulate our way to the high table. But the Bible teaches us that the opposite of selfishly getting what we want is humbly to receive what God gives, and be thankful and content with what He provides.

Jesus contrasted Himself with the proud religious leaders in Matthew 11:29 by saying, *"Take my yoke upon you and learn of me, for I am gentle and humble in heart, and you will find rest for your souls"* (NIV).

A test of leadership is to ask, "Who am I, as a person? Am I gentle and humble, or dominating and proud?" Pride gives a leader an exaggerated sense of his own importance. A leader who walks in genuine humility understands his deficiencies as well as his capabilities. He is willing to share his authority with others so they can be empowered to fulfill God's call for their lives.

> **A leader who walks in genuine humility understands his deficiencies as well as his capabilities.**

A leader often learns to walk in humility by being willing to submit to those in authority. Ask yourself the question: To whom am I submitted? You build on the shoulders of those who have gone on before you because true leaders know not to seek honor, titles, or special treatment. They serve because they are called by God and recognize the need for godly leadership around them.

Separating ourselves or exalting ourselves above others is sectarianism. God hates sectarianism. This spirit that says, "We are right and you are wrong" divides families, nations, cultures, and churches. For example, if we believe our church has the only right doctrine, or has a better model of doing church than others, we can easily fall into pride. There is nothing wrong with being unique and finding what works best for us and our church, but be advised that not everything that works for us will work for everyone else!

The Scripture makes it clear that if you humble yourself under the mighty hand of God, He will exalt you in due time (see 1 Pet. 5:6). God wants to exalt you. He wants to honor you. When are you honored by God? When you humble yourself before Him. If I try to do God's job, if I try to exalt myself, then God will have to do my job. He will have to humble me. I would rather humble myself and allow God to exalt me than exalt myself and have God humble me—wouldn't you?

What Humility Is Not

Humility isn't walking with your head bowed down, trying to look humble. In a quest to be humble, people sometimes confuse humility with false modesty. We've all probably done this if we were to admit it. We are recognized for an accomplishment and when someone praises us, we say, "Oh, it was just something I threw together." We downplay what we've done under the pretense of humility. This really is false pride. False pride can look like humility but is often full of legalistic pride. The following Scripture deals with this kind of false pride. *"Pay careful attention to your own work, for then you will get the satisfaction of a job well done, and you won't need to compare yourself to anyone else"* (Gal. 6:4).

True humility is an attitude of the heart that is constantly acknowledging this truth: that without Jesus we can do nothing, but with Jesus we can do all things (see Phil. 4:13). It is being conscious of our weaknesses and willing to give God all the credit for things we have achieved and accomplished.

> **True humility is an attitude of the heart that is constantly acknowledging this truth: that without Jesus we can do nothing.**

Some people also confuse humility with timidity. Humility is not clothing ourselves in an attitude of self-deprecation or being afraid to attempt things. We can maintain our sense of satisfaction in our achievements without arrogance. We can have a quiet confidence in our leadership without tooting our own horn.

How Do You Maintain Humility?

Success as a leader can sometimes dazzle you, but there's usually someone around to help you keep perspective. I love the story of TV anchorman, Tom Brokaw: Brokaw was wandering through Bloomingdale's department store in New York City one day, shortly after he was promoted to co-host on the *Today Show*. The *Today Show* was a pinnacle for Brokaw after years of work, first in Omaha, then for NBC in Los Angeles and Washington. He was feeling good about himself. He noticed a man watching him closely. The man kept staring at him, and finally when the man approached him, Brokaw was sure he was about to reap the first fruits of being a New York City television celebrity. The man pointed his finger and said, "Tom Brokaw, right?"

"Right," said Brokaw.

"You used to do the morning news on KMTV in Omaha, right?"

"That's right," said Brokaw, getting set for the accolades to follow.

"I knew it the minute I spotted you," the fellow said. Then he paused and added, "Whatever happened to you?"[4]

If we exalt ourselves, God will humble us. Conversely, if we humble ourselves before the Lord, God will exalt us in due time. Humility means handing our sense of our personal power or importance over to God who truly has the real power. We should never forget from where the Lord has brought us. I am still amazed that He has called me to be a Christian leader who travels across the globe training leaders. It is by God's grace, and I will never forget where I was when God called me. We all face the test of humility at some time in our lives. When we pass it, we realize that we have learned to shift the focus away from ourselves and gladly recognize the contributions of others. We don't have the need to pull rank but instead notice other people, even if they seem to be way down at the bottom of the list.

In Rick Warren's book *The Purpose Driven Life*, he says: "Humility is not thinking less of yourself, but thinking of yourself less."[5] Great advice!

—⁓—

Now, back to Anthony, the mega-church youth pastor.

After watching Justin take all the credit for the success of the youth event, Anthony went to God. "God, help me to have the right attitude," he prayed. "Help me not to be driven by the need to get the credit for a job well done. I know you resist the proud, but give grace to the humble. I am going to depend on you to keep me humble." Anthony gained the peace he needed as he submitted to the Lord. He understood that he was no better or more important than any member in the youth department. Pride, rather than humility had reared its ugly head in an attempt to meet an emotional need for significance that Anthony had. Deep inside, Anthony knew that the secret to embracing humility is to embrace the life of Jesus. That meant carrying a cross—not wearing a crown.

Endnotes

1. *Full Life Study Bible* (Grand Rapids, MI: Zondervan, 1992), 1962.

2. "Toward Others, Be Humble," *John Mark Ministries,* http://jmm.aaa.net.au/articles/2267.htm (Accessed February 2009).

3. K. Hughes, *Liberating Ministry From the Success Syndrome* (Carol Stream, IL: Tyndale, 1988), 45.

4. Sermon Central, http://www.sermoncentral.com/SearchResults30.asp?keyword.... (Accessed January 2009).

5. Rick Warren, *Purpose Driven Life* (Grand Rapids, MI: Zondervan, 2002), 265.

The Humility Test

Personal reflection questions/discussion

1. How do you sometimes try to make yourself look good as a leader?

2. Do you understand your deficiencies as well as your capabilities? How is this humbling?

3. In a society that encourages competition and individuality, how can you be humble?

4. How can false pride resemble humility?

5. How can the accountability of friends and relationships around you help with the test of humility?

6. Describe ways to keep your perspective and maintain humility when you experience success as a leader.

Chapter 3

The Teamwork Test

An effective leader finds a way for his team to win.

When Dan stepped into his new position at TR Plastics, the research and development department he was to lead was in shambles. Every time his team sat down at a staff meeting, there was bickering and disagreements. It seemed as if no one knew how to communicate, which made almost everyone feel left in the dark, confused, and misunderstood.

As a seasoned manager, Dan soon saw where the origins of the problems lay. Two members constantly blamed each other for not meeting deadlines. Others on the team felt the need to brag to let people know they did a good job. In general, there was no camaraderie or teamwork taking place. Although the work was getting done, it often happened in a haphazard and chaotic way, causing stress to everyone on the team. And it was not the best work they could do. It was just adequate.

The research and development department had become known as the place where there was a huge vacuum of leadership and where squabbles took precedence over order and harmony.

Dan knew he was not in his leadership position to simply manage the tasks at hand. As a manager, he wanted his team to win and move beyond their problems. He knew that relationships would have to be built—healthier, stronger, honest relationships—so there could be better performance on the job. How could he lead by example and help the employees see the bigger picture and understand how they could contribute to it? How could he create a workplace environment where his team was fully engaged and communicated clearly, serving together as one? It was going to be a challenge, but Dan was prepared to face the test.

Some corporations offer team-building exercises to try to get their employees to learn to work together in a more cohesive fashion. These team-building exercises can be outdoor pursuits such as wilderness-type things like rope climbing or navigating whitewater. I've even heard of one company that offered a team building exercise where teams jump out of an airplane and have to organize themselves in some sort of formation. Needless to say, I would opt out on that type of organizational team-building exercise! I'm not sure risking your life for that kind of working together produces real results.

I do know that God is a team builder. He knows how teams work and how they can effectively work together. God the Father, God the Son, and God the Holy Spirit created the universe. They were a team. When Jesus lived on earth 2000 years ago, He sent His disciples out two by two, in teams. He trained His disciples in a group. As a leader, you can follow His example. Often God uses one person to express the vision and others to turn it into reality. When you encourage and inspire others, you put teamwork into action to accomplish God's goals.

What You Can Do as a Team

Baseball legend Cal Ripken, Jr. was interviewed about his success as a baseball player. Many believe he is one of the greatest players in baseball history, but his individual success was not what mattered most to him. In the interview, he said:

> I'd much rather be referred to not as an individually great player, or someone who tore up the record books, but someone who came to the ball park and said: "Okay, I'm here. I want to play. What can I do to help us win today?" A lot of people ask, "What is your greatest play—your greatest accomplishment?" I say, "I caught the last out of the World Series." It wasn't a great catch—I didn't dive, I didn't do a cartwheel and throw the guy out at first base. People's mouths didn't drop open on the play. We all want to be part of something bigger. But we all have our little jobs that we have to do as a member of a team. Everybody has their individual responsibilities, but they all have to come together for a main goal...So the most fulfilling moment I could ever have, again, was catching the last out of the World Series—knowing *we* did it.[1]

Jesus could have accomplished His work on earth on His own, but He chose to work with a team to fulfill the task. He developed His disciples by giving them intense on-the-job training. He talked with them, prayed with them, affirmed them, warned them, challenged them as a team, and even told them they would do even greater things than He did.

Jesus could have accomplished His work on earth on His own, but He chose to work with a team.

Every Person on the Team Counts!

Sarah, a youth leader from our church, says that she has come to recognize that on the youth teams she has led and been part of over the years, even less mature members can hear from the Lord things she may not be hearing. She is aware that she must listen to her entire team to fully hear from the Lord.

Teamwork is demonstrated for us in the way the Father, Son, and Holy Spirit work together as one, yet each has His own role: God uses teamwork. The early Church appointed elders to work together *"in every town"* (Titus 1:5). They had responsibilities together.

Sometimes a leader may think, "If only I had a more experienced and mature team, we could move full steam ahead." At the same time, the team may be thinking, "If only our leader were a better leader, we could really go somewhere!" Teamwork means that each person on the team is convinced without a shadow of a doubt that every other team member is vital to the team's success. In George Barna's book *Leaders on Leadership,* the word *teamwork* is described as "working together toward the fulfillment of a desired outcome without the loss of one's individuality."[2]

Do you look for people like you when you build a team? That really is not necessary; in fact, it is ill advised because you already have you! Find others to work with you who have the strengths you lack. Some of us can do one task; some can do another. Regardless of our shortcomings or problems, God recognizes each team member as valuable. Each person on the team has something unique to offer, and their differing gifts round out the mix.

Allow each person to use his or her gifts to get specific jobs done. God will put others on a team who can do things much better than the leader. That is exactly what a leader should look for—he wants to find those who, through relationship rather than competition, can resource his weaknesses. I am a blessed man. I serve with various teams of people from around the world, and these team members are amazing. Many of these leaders are much more gifted than I am. Some are better at counseling than I am, others more gifted in administration and finances, others better at problem solving. Still others have found themselves in a position to give counsel to leaders of cities and nations.

> **A leader should look for those who, through relationship rather than competition, can resource his weaknesses.**

A leader was heard saying, "Every act of courage I take is usually sparked by the team around me." Teamwork encourages the team leader to listen to his team, be inspired by them, and remain steadfast so as not to let his team members down.

Find Common Ground

The four commonalities for a team to function well together are vision, values, procedure, and healthy relationships. When team members function as they should—with common vision, common values, and common procedures—they are operating from a place of security and love for each other and a common focus so healthy teamwork can happen.

Members on a team must have common vision to be effective. This means they must all know where they are headed and be in agreement with this direction. But they must also have common values. Values are those things you believe so deeply that you would be willing to die for them. It takes a period of time of serving with someone to begin to see what he or she really values. In addition, there must be common procedures. Common procedures are the practical methods needed to carry out the vision. You must all be in agreement concerning how you will carry out your God-given vision. And you must have healthy relationships. If any of these areas are missing, a team will find itself struggling to function as a team.

The relationships on a team must be God-given, healthy relationships. There are many dreadful stories of leadership teams that have fractured. A church that was going through some relational leadership problems encouraged their pastor to take a vacation and generously sent him to Hawaii. While there he received a call from one of the elders who informed him that he had taken two-thirds of the congregation and started a new church. The remaining congregation was torn apart and never recovered.

There had been a breakdown in relationship simmering under the surface for many months that was never dealt with, and the team was destroyed.

Team members must feel valued and secure in the team environment. They must all realize they have a job to do, and no one can do their job better than they. Healthy leaders will do all they can to create a team environment that encourages each member to function in their particular gifts. A leader should never feel threatened if others on the team are more gifted in certain ministry areas.

The author of this little motto is unknown, but the message is loud and clear: "The best leader is the one who has sense enough to pick good people to get done what he wants done and has self-restraint enough to keep from meddling with them while they do it."

The Importance of Interdependence

The Scriptures speak in Isaiah 54:2 of lengthening our cords and strengthening our stakes (NIV). There is a leadership application here for us to experience. Some of us are created to be *lengtheners* and some of us are born *strengtheners*.

Lengtheners are often visionary leaders who want to see their influence and their teams grow and expand, while strengtheners have a vision to help the team and people grow deeper and become better at what they are doing. Both are needed on a team for it to be effective. I used to think that every leader thought like me! I was wrong. I have learned to appreciate others on the team who are different from me. The key is interdependence. I have found that most persons are strengtheners, but understanding who you are on a team will cause the team to be so much more effective. We need each other. We must learn to be interdependent. Organizational researchers reserve the term *team* for groups that have high interdependence—each task that you do is dependent on what the other team members are doing at that same time.

Dependent people need others to get what they want. Independent people can get what they want through their own effort. Interdependent people combine their own efforts with the efforts of others to achieve the greatest success.[3]

When we are convinced that God has called each person as a member of the team, we are also convinced that each one has something unique to offer to the team. There can be no competition, because others' gifts and personalities bring wholeness to the team. When we understand others' strengths and weaknesses, we can build as a team, capitalizing on strengths and providing support where others are weak.

Tests of Teamwork

In First Chronicles 12:16-17, some leaders who were defecting from Saul came to join up with David. One of David's first questions to them was "Have you come peaceably?" As a leader, he needed to know if there were things in their background or their previous experience that would hinder them. Were they bringing extra baggage to the team, or were they laying everything down at the door?

Another question David asked was, "Have you come to help me?" A supportive leader or team player must lay down any previous vision or agenda of his own and embrace the vision of the team where he is serving. If he is unwilling to do this, it will only be a matter of time until there is more than one vision operating in the team. And with more than one vision, you have "di-vision." David wanted to know if they would support him and support the vision the Lord had given to him.

"Will you betray me to my enemies?" was another question David asked. The shortcomings of individuals may cause them to be disloyal when times get rough. I have worked with a lot of different people, and I have found that no one is perfect! David was asking these men what they would do when they saw his flaws. Similarly, will the leadership team stand and help make up for the weaknesses of their leader, or will they expose them? Will they use his weaknesses as weapons against him by pointing them out or exaggerating them to others?

When the men replied in affirmation and support of David's leadership, David finally replied, "Then my heart will be knit with yours." David then commissioned these men to serve on his team, making them leaders of his raiding bands.

In verse 18, the chief of the captains pledged his loyalty to David, *"We are yours, O David! We are with you, O son of Jesse! Success, success to you, and success to those who help you, for your God will help you"* (1 Chron. 12:18 NIV). When leaders are working together in unity, bonded by commitment and free from hurts of the past, they are bound to experience success. If the team is not focused and in unity about the direction of the team, they will be tested. Good communication and respect for each other through committed relationships will result in successful teamwork.

One Is a Lonely Number

An article printed in *Physician* magazine called attention to the loneliness and discouragement of Church leaders: 80 percent of Church leaders and 84 percent of their spouses feel discouraged or deal with feelings of depression, while more than 40 percent of Church leaders and 47 percent of their spouses suffer from feelings of burnout.[4]

David was a righteous man *"after God's own heart"* (see Acts 13:22) and the anointed king of Israel. Yet even as God's chosen, he found himself one day crying out to the Lord from the dark cave of Adullam (see Ps. 142:1-7). The battle before him was greater than he felt he could handle. It seemed like a desperate and hopeless situation, and there was no one at his right hand to help him. There was no one to stand with him. David felt as if no one cared for him.

This is the picture of many Church leaders today. They feel like they stand alone, and they are discouraged. There is a feeling that they are in Church leadership by themselves, and there is no one who feels what they feel, who hurts the way they hurt, and who bleeds the way they bleed.

"If leadership and loneliness go hand-in-hand, we must form a new union," said Duane Britton, a pastor in one of the churches in our network of churches. In a *Ministry Today* magazine article he wrote, he said:

> In Scripture we find that even Jesus Christ experienced loneliness. John 1:11 says, *"He came to His own, and His own did not receive Him."* Christ established the standard of leadership, yet I don't believe His purpose for coming to this earth was for us—particularly leaders—to remain in self-imposed exile and isolation. We were never meant to become islands unto ourselves.[5]

God's plan never was for a leader to stand alone. The wonderful blessing of a healthy team of leaders is the way it provides the leader with close working relationships. The other leaders on the team rally around the leader to surround, serve, and help him bear the responsibilities of leadership. The Lord is raising up teams who will stand alongside their leader and not shrink back. These teams are willing to go to the battle and not break rank nor be intimidated by the odds against them.

A leader and his team can withstand the force and pressures they face when together they stand firm. They are committed and sold out to their God-given vision and the people to whom the Lord has called them to serve. They will stand together, steadfast in times of trouble, against uncertainty and seemingly insurmountable odds. Being team players means that the members on the team respect and support their leader; however, it does not mean they cannot question him.

Every leader knows that in order to grow in leadership, he must conscientiously welcome suggestions and criticisms from the team. We are tested as leaders when we receive constructive criticism from a team member and are tempted to become angry and would like to "put him in his place." We simply need to ask God for His grace so we can position ourselves for these times and stay humble and teachable. It is much more important to be Christ-like than it is to be right. If the criticism is unfounded, we can then correct the team member in gentleness and kindness, displaying the fruit of the Spirit.

Working Together for Each Other's Benefit

Phil Vischer, the creator of *VeggieTales,* in his book *Me, Myself, & Bob,* tells the story of how Walt Disney and his brother Roy worked together as a team. He describes how Walt was the dreamer and Roy the practical one in their partnership. Roy did not always like the great ideas of Walt, but he loved Walt and believed in him. Walt knew he couldn't do what Roy did, and Roy knew he couldn't do what Walt did. So they submitted to each other's area of expertise and worked together, ultimately for the benefit of the ideas and the benefit of their audience.

> If God has given you ideas for ministry, look for your Roy. It may not be one person—your Roy may be several people or even a whole board of directors. But the relationship will work only if the people you bring in to perform that role are there because they want to see your ideas succeed—want to see you succeed.
>
> If on the other hand, God has made you a Roy, look for your Walt. Look for someone with creative giftings and calling. That person needs you desperately.[6]

You and I can learn a lesson from Paul, the apostle, who was one of the greatest leaders to have ever lived and was tremendously used by God. He never chose to work alone. He surrounded himself with capable people who would share his vision, devotion, and willingness to work with others. A good leader will pass the leadership test when he understands he cannot work alone, but make every effort to listen to and interact and work with others on his team.

—⚬—

Remember Dan?

It was not easy for Dan, but as the new research and development department manager at his company, he took the time to listen to each member on his team. At staff meetings, he encouraged each person to listen to their co-workers, even if they thought it was the silliest idea they had ever heard. When each team member started considering the group's ideas and not just their own, they started to gel as a group. Leading by example and treating others respectfully, Dan created enthusiasm on the team. In fact, Dan's team became known as the department team that was committed not only to making their projects work well, but also to have a strong bond of relationship and camaraderie while doing so. Dan never took any of the credit for what had happened. He gave the credit to the team.

Endnotes

1. Sermon Central, http://www.sermoncentral.com/SearchResults30 .asp.

2. George Barna, *Leaders on Leadership* (Ventura, CA: Regal Books, 1997), 214.

3. Stephen R. Covey, *The Seven Habits of Highly Effective People* (New York, NY: Free Press, A Division of Simon & Schuster, Inc., 1989), 49.

4. Dr. James Dobson, "The Titanic. The Church. What They Have in Common," http://www2.focusonthefamily.com/docstudy/newsletters/ A000000803.cfm, (Accessed July 29, 2009).

5. Duane Britton, "Islands Unto Ourselves," *Ministry Today*, May-June 2009, 62.

6. Phil Vischer, *Me, Myself, & Bob* (Nashville, TN: Thomas Nelson, 2006), 213-214.

The Teamwork Test

Personal reflection questions/discussion

1. What can we learn from Jesus' example of how teams work together through His relationship with the 12 disciples?

2. Describe the commonalities all teams must have. Do you have these functioning on your team? If not, how can they begin to be built?

3. As a leader, how do you find ways for your team to win?

4. How does interdependence work on your team?

5. How do you communicate and problem solve on your team? Do you give respect to others? Do you demand it for yourself?

6. What happens within you when a team member gives direct criticism or seems to resist the direction of the team?

—⚏—

Chapter 4

The Releasing Test

An effective leader knows how to empower others.

Seven years ago, Emily had not seen herself as the kind of person who might lead her church's women's ministry. She was not particularly outgoing or charismatic, but she felt called to lead the women at Bethany Church, and it evolved from there. She grew to love the women, and over the years she was inspired by their determination to grow spiritually.

She became a good leader almost by default and was grateful to God for the grace He had given her. She felt humbled to be a part of God's transforming power in the lives of these women and of His plan for their lives. With a heart for God and a love for people, Emily made herself available with timely and godly advice. She wanted to see these women grow spiritually, and she found ways to encourage and develop godliness in the women.

She also took seriously her role in mentoring a team of women around her. She realized that mentoring and growing leaders who would eventually be ready to take on new challenges and opportunities goals were of any good leader. So she was not surprised when Sophia asked to start her own women's group for career women in the church. It really made sense; the women's group was getting too large. Smaller groups of women meeting together would alleviate the extensive planning needed for the large group.

Sophia had great leadership qualities. She was friendly, encouraging, and never spoke a bad word about anyone. She was confident in her strengths, yet had the willingness to learn from others. Organization was her strong suit. She had helped Emily for a year and had kept everything in the women's ministry running like a well-oiled machine. In fact, the women's ministry had grown exponentially in a very short time, and much of it could be attributed to Sophia's leadership and people skills.

There was no doubt that Sophia was a great leader. In fact, Emily thought, *she really is far more gifted than I am in so many ways.* Although Emily recognized that fact, she suddenly found herself feeling uncharitable toward Sophia and her many gifts. She noticed that Sophia was garnering a lot of attention from the ladies. Many seemed drawn to her and her charisma. *"Hadn't I been the one to lay the groundwork for the women's ministry?"* Emily thought. *"I put so many years and hours into this ministry, and what if all the women gravitate toward the new group? I'd be left with a few old ladies!"* Emily faced a dilemma. Would she practice what she preached and graciously release Sophia to step out on her own? Would she pass the test?

—⁂—

Making room for new leaders must be an intentional goal for a leader. There is a great need for leaders of all kinds to reproduce themselves and release those they have trained to fly on their own. Leaders reproduce themselves by mentoring others. They will do everything they can to help others fulfill their visions and dreams and then release them to achieve their goals!

The Corinthian Church needed spiritual fathers (and mothers), according to First Corinthians 4:15. Paul scolded them for not becoming spiritual parents so they could reproduce themselves.

> *For even if you had ten thousand others to teach you about Christ, you have only one spiritual father. For I became your father in Christ Jesus when I preached the Good News to you.* (1 Corinthians 4:15)

These believers lacked parents or mentors to give them proper training and nurturing. They needed help to put their knowledge into life practice.

It was the year 1980 in Harlem when a business leader gave some young children hope to see their dreams realized. His fatherly encouragement carried them forward and set them on a path to go beyond what they ever imagined they could.

Eugene Lang, a self-made multi-millionaire, stood before a group of 61 sixth graders graduating from elementary school. He had been asked to come and speak to them about how he had once sat in the same auditorium where they were almost fifty years earlier and that they too could achieve what he had. But before he got up to speak, he realized that his speech was nothing short of balderdash. Most of these students were Hispanic or African American and lived well below the poverty line. The drop out rate at the high school that many of them would be attending was astronomical. So the likelihood of any of these students being able to reproduce his success was nothing short of impossible. Instead of speaking his quasi-inspirational message that morning, he stood before them to say that he was setting aside $2,000 for each of them to go to college and for every consecutive year that they stayed in school he would increase that amount. Five years later, 52 of those 61 were in the 11th grade and were meeting with Mr. Lang to discuss where they would attend college. You see, many of these kids had written off the chance to go to college from an early age because they knew that their parents could not afford it. They had no hope of going to college, so why even try to do well in high school? But, Mr. Lang had given them hope. He had made a way where there has been none.[1]

Leaders will not only release others, but they will empower them to succeed. Jesus, the ultimate Leader, gave His inexperienced disciples His trust and confidence when He placed the responsibility for establishing His Church in their hands. Like these students, they were unlikely prospects, but He trusted them to do great things as He released them into leadership.

Leaders will not only release others, but they will empower them to succeed.

Attentive leaders are those who can spot potential in others. They can look at someone and see the dreams inside of them regarding what they can become for Jesus Christ. Sometimes, the dreams are locked up for some reason, perhaps because of immaturity or fear. People need others who will help them unlock their dreams and then release them to use their gifts.

Natural as well as spiritual parents are wise to recognize they have a great responsibility to help their children do even greater things than they have. My friend Steve's son, Marc, is a born drummer. They have pictures of him at age two playing drums on pots and pans with wooden spoons. His first drum set was a cartoon character toy set from his grandparents. Marc beat those drums until they fell to pieces. As a young man, Steve was also a drummer, and he would have had to be a blind and deaf father not to realize his son's potential as a drummer.

Steve recalls, "We started with a practice pad and finally a single snare drum. Marc learned the rudiments of drumming on those two instruments. He begged me for a 'real' drum set, but the time had not yet come." Sometimes as spiritual fathers, we want our children to go from pots and pans to the whole set almost instantly, but it is premature.

Eventually, when the rudiments became second nature to Marc, Steve passed on to Marc his vintage drum set. Marc was ready for lessons that took him beyond a single snare drum.

Today, in a traveling band, Marc has far surpassed Steve in drumming. If Steve had tried to hold him back to his own level, he would be a selfish, insecure parent. A secure parent releases his children, encouraging his sons or daughters to excel to greater heights than he ever did. Parents get under their children and find out what is in their hearts and help them fulfill their own vision. And by the way, parents do not necessarily do everything for their children, but they help find those who can serve as resources to them.

How Will We Release Them?

Leaders, like parents, give those they are leading the tools they need to be well-rounded individuals who can become effective leaders on their own. Leaders must think of their spiritual sons and daughters they have mentored and trained as belonging to the Lord. The Lord has a purpose and calling for that son or daughter. A leader must be willing to release them into their calling as they come to maturity. Only a dysfunctional parent would try to keep his son or daughter at home to help him fulfill his own vision. Of course, this is a test that tests our personal security.

My friend Brian played baseball in tenth grade in high school. But in the eleventh grade, he was cut from the team. Now that Brian has sons of his own, should he force them to play baseball and in this way fulfill his own unfulfilled dreams of being a great baseball player? Of course not! His sons might enjoy playing soccer or basketball or the guitar instead. He will encourage them to fulfill whatever dreams they have in their hearts. Proverbs 22:6 states, *"Train a child in the way he should go, and when he is old he will not turn from it"* (NIV).

The emphasis here is on the way *he* should go, not the way *his father or mother thinks* he should go. Of course, children need training in areas of morality and character. But when it comes to personal vision and calling, a parent's job is to find out what God has put in their children's hearts.

Rick Joyner spoke to pastors in our city several years ago and pointed out that it is not old, gray-haired men and women who have children. It is usually young men and women, perhaps in their 20s and 30s, who conceive and give birth to children and become natural parents. Rick spoke prophetically when he warned the Church not to "sterilize" or "neuter" the young stallions, referring to the young leaders that God is anointing and giving to our local churches. Seasoned leaders must release younger leaders to serve in roles of leadership that fit their personality and style. Let's be sure we do not expect them to do things exactly the same way we have done them; otherwise, they end up wearing "Saul's armor," as young David experienced (see 1 Sam. 17:38-40). David preferred a slingshot, and the rest is history!

As leaders we must learn to listen to the voice of God, but also teach potential leaders to hear from the Lord. We must release them to hear from the Lord for themselves. This will cause potential leaders to look to God for revelation and direction instead of depending on the leaders in an unhealthy way. In addition, it takes some of the spiritual pressure off of the present leadership when other leaders are hearing from God for themselves.

Elijah trained others as he learned to hear God's voice. While Elijah was depressed and living in a cave, he found that God was not in the wind, the earthquake, or the fire, but spoke through a still, small voice. The Lord told him to anoint Elisha, a prophet, in his place (see 1 Kings 19:16). For the remainder of his life, Elijah trained Elisha and other young prophets. He was a spiritual father to them. The fathering grew out of his own walk with the Lord as he learned to hear God's voice clearly. Like He did with Elijah, God has granted us the priceless privilege of fellowship with Himself as we train others and release them to fulfill the Lord's call on their lives. If you are interested in learning more about how to practically become a spiritual father or mother and release the next generation of leadership, I have written much more on this subject in my book *The Cry for Spiritual Fathers and Mothers.*[2]

Let's allow our talented young leaders to pave their own way in the world.

Let's allow our talented young leaders to pave their own way in the world. Allow them to leave in order to pioneer new things on their own. When we train a person in a skill or ministry, they must be free to move on to start their own business or ministry if they are called by God to do so. We must train them to release them! If we truly release them, it is OK if they do it differently than we would have. This is the test of releasing.

—⟢—

As a spiritual mother, Emily knew that she had done the right thing by multiplying herself in developing Sophia as a leader. Every good parent wants to raise up healthy, successful children. In fact, parents delight in helping prepare their children so they can go far beyond them in gifts and talents and become even more successful. Because Emily allowed Sophia room to spread her wings and fly, the women's ministry became so much more effective as it expanded to include diverse smaller groups. Emily did not want to miss out on the amazing work God was doing in the women's ministry. It was not about her, after all. The joy of seeing women connect with each other was reward enough. From now on, she knew she could completely release other women into leadership roles as they started other groups. She had passed the "releasing test."

Endnotes

1.   Sermon Central, http://www.sermoncentral.com/SearchResults30.asp (Accessed January 2009).

2.   Larry Kreider, *The Cry for Spiritual Fathers and Mothers*, (Lititz, PA: House to House Publications, 2000).

The Releasing Test

Personal reflection questions/discussion

1. Are you a leader who can spot potential in others? How?

2. How are you making room for new leaders in your organization?

3. Are you secure enough in your leadership to trust others to carry on with the work that you've started?

4. How have you personally helped a young leader break through to new levels of ministry potential?

5. How many potential leaders are you currently mentoring, and who are they mentoring?

6. How is releasing young leaders directly correlated to spiritual mothering and fathering?

—⁂—

Chapter 5

The Priorities Test

*An effective leader determines what his
priorities are in life.*

Like many pastors, William from Open Door Church wore many hats. His life was filled with reading, studying, sermon preparation, preaching, visiting the sick, counseling, and officiating at weddings, funerals, and nursing home services. His calendar was filled with an unending stream of meetings, appointments, and conferences, committee meetings, Bible studies, prayer groups, church suppers, hospital visits, and home visits. Additionally, as the senior pastor, his job was to oversee the administration and management of all areas of the congregation's ministry. It seemed he was never off-duty. He was literally on the job 24/7.

Lately William had been feeling exhausted, but he felt guilty about saying "no" to any legitimate request on his time, so he just continued to fill his schedule to the max. There were always a hundred essential tasks that he was certain would never get done unless he did them himself. People expected him to be a pillar of strength, but he knew he was not eating right or getting enough sleep. He was irritable at home, couldn't relax, and couldn't remember the last time he and his wife took a real vacation.

He knew he needed to take time off for himself and his family, but there was always more work to be done, one more phone call to make, one more sermon to prepare. William knew he was burning the candle at both ends, but surely God would honor his commitment and hard work. He was facing the test of priorities.

—m—

William was a leader who had a mistress in his life—the mistress of ministry. Anything, even a really good thing that means more to us than Jesus, is idolatry. A mistress of ministry takes us away from the simplicity of devotion to Christ.

First John 5:21 tells us to stay away from idols, and Ezekiel 14:3 speaks of those who have idols in their hearts. Often the idols in our hearts are those things we seek for joy and significance. Pastor Tim Keller, tells a story about a time when he discovered this application in his own life.

> I came home one Wednesday evening (after a church session meeting) whistling with joy over the unity of the elders and the success I had dealing with complex problems. When I entered the house my wife said, "Wow, Tim, you must have had a great day." I suddenly recognized that my moods had less to do with the nature and character and promises of God, than whether I got what I wanted at work. I had to think of the words of John Calvin, who said, "Our hearts are idol factories. What do you worship?"[1]

If we want the Lord to speak to us and guide us, our hearts cannot be filled with desires that rise above our love for Jesus. The elders of Israel were guilty of idolatry in their hearts. God refused to answer their prayers anymore because they desired an ungodly way of life (see Ezek. 14:3).

If something means more to us than Jesus, it is idolatry. Idols in our lives may be our churches, ministries, job, corporation, or even our families. If a leader's employment or ministry takes first priority in his life, it is an idol. God wants our first love. He wants to be the first in our desires before our ministries. If we are in love with a method or philosophy of business or ministry, it is an idol. Only Jesus is worthy of our true worship and full devotion.

In the early 1980s, I served with a group of young leaders as we started a new church in Lancaster County, Pennsylvania. Our new church began with much excitement. Pouring all of our energies into this new work, we discussed, thought, and dreamed about "our vision." Eventually it dawned on us that we were exalting our vision above Jesus. I was so convicted by the Lord when I read in First John 5:21 that we are to keep ourselves from idols. Jesus shares His glory with no other, not even a good vision. This was probably the biggest mistake we ever made as a church! We repented for exalting our vision above Jesus.

Although we continued to believe that having a clear vision is a successful strategy for church growth, we also recognized that we can never allow a vision, no matter how good it is, to take the place of Christ's preeminence in our ministries, workplaces, or lives.

Expose the Idols and Pass the Test!

The human heart is never neutral; it must worship something. It longs to attach to something. Whether we want to admit it or not, the heart is often an idol factory elevating things or people above God. It happens so subtly. For example, when you are worried, where do you look for comfort or security, other than to your heavenly Father? Do you look to yourself—to your own mind and intellect? Do you look to your education, money, status, home, family, friends, beauty, or image?

By going after these idols or "other lovers" you are saying to God,

"Jesus is not enough. I also need to be recognized for my accomplishments to be happy. I need power over others in order to be happy. I need to be loved and respected by my friends in order to be happy. I need to have a particular body image to be happy. I need to be highly productive and get a lot of things done to be happy. I need to be free of money worries to be happy." These are all idols of the heart that, as leaders, we must recognize and tear down.

Let's be familiar with what we set our hearts on, what motivates us, what controls us, and what we serve with our energy and resources. We may be surprised by what we find. Our idols may emerge as a desire for attention, an attachment to comfort, a demand for people to meet our needs, or a compulsion to work.

God wants to help us expose those idols of our heart so we can be like the early believers who, "...*turned to God from...idols to serve* [the living and true] *God Who is alive and true and genuine*" (1 Thess. 1:9 AMP). God wants our total and complete love and obedience. In the Old Testament, the problem with the golden calf was not that it was a statue of gold, but that it became the Israelites' substitute for God. Idolatry of any kind seeks to replace God in our lives.

God's First!

Your priorities reveal the things you value most in life. What you value you will prioritize, and what you prioritize you will invest in. Jesus said the same thing when He stated that *"Wherever your treasure is, there the desires of your heart will also be"* (Matt. 6:21).

What you value you will prioritize, and what you prioritize you will invest in.

Some Christian leaders make a list of priorities in an attempt to better order their lives and keep their priorities straight. Their list often looks like this: God, family, church, work. Although this list seems accurate, the number-one priority, with no exceptions, is that God wants to be first place in our lives. When we place Him first in our lives, all the other areas of life will work together because we are listening to God's voice daily and obeying Him first.

God being first place in your life means that His wishes come before yours. Your relationship to God spills out into all your other relationships. Only when your vertical relationship to God is authentic can your horizontal relationships with other people be genuine. As God's importance in your life spills out into your other relationships, you will notice that your family life, church life, and life at your job improves. So making God your first priority means that you will put your spouse's desires above your own, you'll have an unselfish attitude toward your children, you'll have a noncritical attitude toward your brothers and sisters in Christ, and you'll be able to show the love of Christ to those at your workplace. You see, making God the number-one priority in your life will affect all the other areas of your life.

> ## Making God the number-one priority in your life will affect all the other areas of your life.

Many of us have the choice daily of whether we will put *people* first or *things* first. Shall we return that phone call or continue with our "to do" list? Things will pass away, but people are eternal beings. Always invest in them first!

Find Balance in Life

Do we make time for those things that are most important in life? We must have a rhythm in life and leadership. We must have the proper balance between God, family, work, and rest. As leaders, there are so many aspects of life that can get out of balance. When we recognize that God must be our top priority, and we spend daily time with Him, something amazing takes place in our hearts. The love of God seems to overwhelm our hearts, and God enables us to walk in this radical thing called *love*.

That love spills out to all of our relationships and helps us to find that balance we need in our lives.

In his book, *The Rhythm of Life*, Richard Exley states that there are four areas of life that must be in rhythm or balance: work, worship, play, and rest.[2] A leader needs to balance these areas of life, all the while recognizing that worshiping God must be top priority.

Work

Our work is a good and godly thing. Adam and Eve were assigned a job in tending the Garden. Leaders, however, often try to accomplish more than is humanly possible! The number one reason leaders have too much to do is that they only feel good about themselves if they are involved in a lot of activity. If completing more work is somehow better, then we can justify taking shortcuts to get things done. This rationalization leads to ethical compromise and character flaws, and it is a trap. Jesus' yoke is easy and His burden is light. Life is meant to be a joy, although of course it has its challenges in order for us to grow. This is true if we are preaching or fixing refrigerators. We must learn to find balance in our work.

Worship

Regular disciplines of prayer, Scripture study, fasting, meditation, solitude, and corporate worship lead to an abundant spiritual life. Taking a walk on the beach with your spouse and watching the sun set also qualifies as worship! Live a lifestyle of lavish worship and appreciation to the Father.

Play

If you feel guilty when you relax, then you have a problem. Proverbs 17:22 teaches us that *"a cheerful heart is good medicine...."* In our culture today, we experience emotional tiredness; it comes from the inside out. This is unlike our grandparents, who experienced physical tiredness. It came from the outside in because they were plowing fields and beating rugs all day long. Play gives us refreshment from emotional tiredness.

Rest

In Exodus 34:21 we find the "Sabbath principle." It speaks of times of rest and reflection and seasons of emotional release. For example, a pastor who works most of the day on Sunday needs to have a Sabbath day off during the week. When Ronald Reagan was president of the United States, he would chop wood when he had free time. Why? Did they need wood to burn in the White House? Of course not! It helped him to relax and detach from his responsibilities. It helped him keep his perspective on leadership and make better decisions. Others will play golf or read books or mow their lawn.

In his book, *Healthy Leaders*, Keith Yoder says that a leader...

> must learn to detach himself from the burdens, emotions, struggles, weights, conflicts, pressures, weariness, and the monotony of leading the group. Detachment is important because a leader needs to be able to back off from his responsibilities and take a fresh look at them.[3]

As a leader, you continually face the challenge of setting and keeping priorities in order. It is too easy to become off balanced and discover you are facing a serious misalignment of priorities. When I was a young pastor, I felt responsible to pour my life into our new church. One weekend my wife and I hosted a guest speaker, Paul Johansson, who had served as the president of Elim Bible College in Lima, New York. He had spent years as a missionary to Africa, and was a revered Christian leader. We felt so honored to have him with us. He spent time with me and my wife LaVerne and with the leaders of our new church. After our day with Paul was nearly over, I asked him for any advice that he might have for me. I will never forget his response. "You do not need to die for the church," he said, "Jesus died for the church." Then he said, "Your responsibility is to die for your wife." I have never forgotten this wise advice.

Our spouses and families are precious gifts from the Father and need to be priorities in our lives. First Timothy 5:8 tells us clearly that *"Those who won't care for their relatives, especially those in their own household, have denied the true faith. Such people are worse than unbelievers."*

Keeping and developing priorities that honor God is essential to the Christian life. As Christian men and women in business or church endeavors, we cannot allow our budget allocations, committee agendas, programs, and fund raising to take the lion's share of our time. We must learn to also reach out to be the salt and light to a broken, hurting world and to keep God first in our lives. Keeping a close tab on our priorities provides a way of walking circumspectly before God.

Let's look at our lives honestly and lay aside all those things that come before God. And let's be careful to not lose our focus.

—ᴍ—

Pastor William finally came to the realization that God expected him to live within the physical and emotional limits God built into him. As a pastor, his priorities had become convoluted, and he needed to make some changes. For too long he had been a workaholic, driven to prove his worth through success as a pastor. He did not want to burnout or drop out, so he decided to take drastic measures to restore his emotional health.

He initiated a regular day off to relax and recharge his batteries. During these times, he spent time with the Lord and worked at keeping a healthy relationship with his wife and children. He developed a regular exercise program and started to eat more healthfully. He made sure he was accountable to a small circle of friends, and they became his personal support network. He set aside time for meditation, prayer, and personal Bible study. As much as possible, he delegated activities to other capable leaders in the church. He found a proper balance between his family, worship, work, and rest and knew he was now passing the "priorities test."

Endnotes

1. http://www.sermoncentral.com/SearchResults30.asp (Accessed July 29, 2009).

2.   Richard Exley, *The Rhythm of Life* (Tulsa, OK: Honor Books, 1987).

3.   Keith Yoder, *Healthy Leaders* (Lititz, PA: House to House Publications, 1998), 45.

The Priorities Test

Personal reflection questions/discussion

1. What is your number one priority as a Christian leader?

2. What "idols" can leaders have in their lives?

3. Describe how you find balance in your life as a leader. Describe a time you were out-of-balance.

4. How do your priorities reveal what you value in life?

5. How much of your typical day is given over to work? To play? To rest? Where do you need to adjust your priorities?

—⚏—

Chapter 6

The Transition Test

*An effective leader understands and leads
the process of change.*

About ten years into the life of our new church, storms began to mount. An undercurrent was surfacing that sapped those in leadership of strength and vision. As the senior leader, I found myself increasingly making decisions that were based more on the desires of others than on what I really believed was the Lord's direction for us as a church.

People began to leave, not in vast numbers, but one family at a time. Even some of those who served in areas of leadership were leaving to find new direction in their lives. More and more I felt pressed into a mold that was not the original vision God had given us. Early on as a church, we believed the Lord was calling us to train and invest in people, so we had the expectation that many believers serving in our church would be empowered to eventually start their own ministries and churches. We realized the importance of constantly training people in order to give them away.

But we had become sidetracked. We found ourselves becoming more and more frustrated and distracted by the many voices around us. Something had to change. We had lost our way.

After taking some extended time away to pray, it became clear to us that in order for our church, DOVE Christian Fellowship, to accomplish what God had in mind for us, we needed to be willing to decentralize our church into eight smaller churches and release each new congregation to its own leadership and calling. We needed to transition from one large church to become a family of self-governing churches which better suited our goal of mobilizing and empowering God's people. In this way, everyone—individuals, families, small groups, and congregations—could fulfill His purposes at the grassroots level.

This would be a huge transition for us as a church of 2000 people. I enjoyed being the senior pastor of a mega-church and the security it brought. Those of us on the leadership team and staff would have to walk in a new level of faith. The finances we had received each week from the tithes of this one local church would now be given to each self-governing church. In some ways, it was almost like starting over.

Would I pass the transition test as a leader and lead the process of change? There were so many things to consider. Would I trust God and remain steadfast?

—⁂—

Whether in the Church, family, or workplace, times of transition are often difficult. Change is rarely easy. Change begins when something ends—it can involve pain and grief, but it's necessary. When change occurs, people often go through a painful grieving process of denial, anger, depression, and a feeling of loss as they struggle to give up the old and accept the new. I often share with pastors that they should remember at times it takes God 20 years or more to get our attention concerning something in our lives that He wants to change, so we should not expect those in the church to "get it" in a month.

A key to a healthy transition is for leaders to not move too fast. They must give people time to go through changes. I grew up on a farm and recall driving a truckload of potatoes in from the fields. If I traveled too fast or turned too sharply, the potatoes went bouncing off the truck. People will "bounce off the truck" if we make abrupt decisions during transitional times in the Church and in business.

A key to a healthy transition is for leaders to not move too fast.

Both those responding to a transition and leading a transition will face tests. A leader will help his group manage the spectrum of their emotions. There is loss felt. There is disappointment. There are a lot of questions that emerge from these changes. A leader will value the people he or she leads. And a leader will communicate, communicate, communicate as he or she leads in the process of change.

We must try to understand the emotions people feel during transition. For some, it feels as if something has died. Often it is their vision of what they expected the church or organization to be. When it changes, they may be unprepared for it. A church leader must realize the importance of teaching the church values during a transition. Vision can change, but the values stay the same because they are based on the Word of God. If people see it in the Bible, they will have faith to endure the change.

Likewise, the people responding to the transition should listen carefully to what their hearts are experiencing and how God desires to work there. Transition brings us into a vulnerable place, but the Lord loves to minister to us there.

When people experience healthy leadership decisions being made by healthy leaders, it allows them to place trust in their leaders. If too many changes happen too quickly, the trust can disappear. It is like keeping money in a bank account—too many withdrawals will lower the balance. Leaders must be aware of the balance in their trust accounts. They must maintain credit in their "trust accounts." It is not a good policy to make major changes in the church when the "trust account" is low. Keep credit in your "trust account," remembering the process is more important than the end result. Give people time to go through the process.

A Successful Transition

A transition happened in the early Church when the Church needed help with the distribution of food to needy families. In Acts 6:1-7, we read that the apostles realized they were spending far too much time attending to the mundane affairs of the Church and did not have enough time for prayer and the preaching of the Word. This situation required that the leaders take a new look at what they could do to alleviate this burden. They transitioned out of doing all the work themselves when they appointed deacons to help them. The change worked well for the Church and allowed its leaders to be more fruitful.

Wise leaders find ways to value the people they serve when leading them through a time of change.

They drew the people into the process by asking them to *"select seven men who are well respected and are full of the Spirit and wisdom. We will give them this responsibility"* (Acts 6:3). Wise leaders will always find ways to value the people whom they serve by including them in the process, especially when leading them through a time of change. This is a test for many leaders who have the right vision but integrate the wrong process.

Lessons Learned in Transition

Phil Vischer tells the story of building and then witnessing the fall of his media empire *VeggieTales*. A couple of the lessons he learned after the company went bankrupt are valuable lessons for leaders to remember as they go through times of transition.

One lesson he learned was that a leader must "know yourself." You must know your strengths and weaknesses. You must know where you should look to others for help and where others should look to you for help.

Another lesson he learned was that "bigger is no longer better." He says, "Real impact today comes from building great relationships, not huge organizations. More overhead equals less flexibility to pursue unexpected opportunities."

In other words, having a healthy relationship with those you serve is so important. As well, the process you take may be more important than just trying to grow a big company or a big institution or a big church. Remember, Jesus changed the world with 12 men.

Vischer also learned that a leader should "build a team that rows in the same direction." He realized that not all his executives were on the same page with their mission and values for the company. When the team is not on the same page, it leads to a confused and dysfunctional workplace.[1]

Godly Takeover!

Deuteronomy 34 tells the story of a leadership transition. It's the story of Moses turning over the leadership reins of the Israelites to Joshua (see Num. 27:12-23). This was no small deal. Moses was a star. He was a revered and famous leader of which the Bible says, *"there has never been another prophet in Israel like Moses…"* (Deut. 34:10-12). He performed miracles and wonders in Egypt when he went singlehandedly to an extremely powerful leader and demanded the release of 2 million slaves. He split a sea and then drowned an army. The Lord spoke to him face-to-face.

Do you think it was easy for Joshua to take over for a star like Moses? Not likely. Looking at it from a natural perspective, Moses was a tough act to follow. Joshua had to have been wondering what kind of leader he would be. He had big shoes to fill. I doubt if he thought, "Well, finally, it's what I deserve; now I can really get things done my way." He probably had serious doubts about whether he could be as effective a leader as Moses was.

But God saw something in Joshua. He was chosen because he had been Moses' companion, supporter, and apprentice. He had already learned leadership skills on the job. He was faithful and wholehearted. Moses encouraged him many times to be courageous. Joshua passed the test of transition with flying colors!

Change is inevitable. It will come. Will we dig in our feet and keep producing "widgets" the way we always have? Or will we lead the way to finding new, more efficient ideas and ways to do things?

—⁂—

It took more than two years of preparing for the transition, but on January 1, 1996, our one large church in Pennsylvania became eight self-governed churches, each with its own leadership team. We formed a leadership team we called an Apostolic Council to give spiritual oversight to DOVE Christian Fellowship International (DCFI), and I was asked to serve as its international director.

Transitioning from one mega-church into eight smaller churches was a radical change. Releasing the people and the elders took time, but it was worth the effort. Of course, during the transition time we had our ups and downs. Some people thought I moved too fast and some people thought I moved too slowly.

As the newly appointed international director, I needed to meet with my leadership team while keeping the entire church in the loop at the same time. We held town meetings; we produced a specific publication that described the changes that would happen; we developed leadership teams in the eight smaller churches—leaders who would help the local churches to work through the major changes. We tried to do everything we could so that the people would feel like they were a part of the process. We made every effort to process the information in a timely and straightforward manner.

And God was with us! He led us every step of the way. Since the transition, we experienced the faithful provision of the Lord again and again as we walked in obedience to Him. Our transition allowed the old structure to die so we could experience the new—a network of churches partnering together throughout the world. At the time of this printing, there are currently more than 150 churches partnering with the DCFI family from the nations of Barbados, Brazil, Bulgaria, Canada, Colombia, DR Congo, Guatemala, Haiti, India, Ireland, Kenya, Myanmar, Netherlands, Peru, Philippines, Rwanda, Scotland, South Africa, Uganda, USA, and Zambia. The Lord has taken us on an amazing journey during the past few years. And by His amazing grace, we passed the test of transition!

Endnote

1.   Phil Vischer, *Me, Myself, & Bob,* (Nashville, TN: Thomas Nelson, 2006), 218, 222.

The Transition Test

Personal reflection questions/discussion

1. How can you include people in the process when going through a time of transition?

2. What are some of the emotions people go through during times of transition, and what can you, as a leader, do to help with these emotions?

3. How can trust be broken between leaders and those they serve during transition?

4. Why is it important that a leader "knows himself" during a transition time?

5. How can a leader have the right vision for change but the wrong process?

6. Someone once said that the only constant in life is change. How does change affect you? Do you embrace or resist change?

—⚌—

Chapter 7

The Criticism Test

*An effective leader accepts criticism and grows in
the process.*

Tom was well-respected as a leader in his community and known around the world as an international speaker and founder of a well-known Christian non-profit organization. One day, after returning home from an overseas trip, his board informed him that they were taking over the organization which Tom had founded. One of the outspoken and stronger board members had seduced the others into believing lies about Tom, convincing them that he was unfit for leadership. The man convinced the others that his actions were for the best and that he would implement discipline to preserve Tom and his ministry. Although the accusing board member never really defined exactly what it was that Tom had done, wild rumors circulated and ran rampant. Tom's reputation was destroyed by innuendo. Since the Lord told him not to defend himself by seeking legal action for this false allegation, Tom chose to resign and walk away. Tom was devastated, but chose not to strike back.

Finally, months later at a meeting of the board and other outside leaders, the accusing member was discovered to be lying about the accusations. But it was too late. The people affected were confused and distraught. Finances slowed down to a trickle. After several months, the thriving non-profit organization closed its doors. Twenty years of ministry, including all the resources of ministry—the building, equipment, books—was lost.

How did Tom react? Would he pass the test of criticism where false accusations ran rampant?

—⁓—

False accusations are the worst kinds of criticism to deal with. But sometimes leaders just have to "drink the cup of bitter water," whether they are innocent or guilty, and allow God to vindicate them. What do I mean by this?

In the Old Testament, if a man had suspicions that his wife was adulterous, he could bring her before the Priest to determine her guilt or innocence. She had to drink holy water with the dust from the tabernacle floor mixed in. If she were guilty, she would become ill and never bear children. If she were innocent, she would be cleared of guilt and able to have children (see Num. 5:11-28). Whether she was innocent or guilty, she had to drink the bitter cup, because God was her only vindicator. This is how it is for us when we are misunderstood. God will vindicate us.

There are two types of ministry before the throne of God: Jesus' ministry of intercession and satan's ministry of accusation. These same two "ministries" can be found in the Church. As leaders we must be the kind who extend Jesus' ministry of intercession to others. If we are falsely accused, we must extend forgiveness. Truth will triumph. We do not have to defend ourselves. Instead, we should focus on the Lord and His presence in our lives. He will vindicate.

But what about those times when, in the early Church, the believers were often falsely accused by those who were not followers of Jesus? Peter told the believers that they should *"...always be prepared to give an answer to everyone who asks you to give the reason for the hope you have. But do this with gentleness and respect"* (1 Pet. 3:15 NIV). In light of some false accusations, we should be ready to give a defense. But only with gentleness and respect as the Holy Spirit directs us.

My nephew Jon, newly graduated from college and applying for a high school teaching position, received an ominous notice from the Department of Transportation. "This is an official notice of suspension of your driving privileges as a result of your conviction of violating the vehicle code DUI general impairment." In addition to the suspended driver's license, the letter gave notice of a prison term requirement for the drunk driving violation. The only problem was that Jon had never received a DUI citation. Yet the Bureau of Driver Licensing had his name, address and birth date on an official notice of suspension. As it turned out, the DUI culprit was someone with the same last name and birth date. A computer program had attached Jon's name and address with someone else's citation in another city. It caused Jon anxiety for a time, but he was polite and respectful in his many calls and visits to the bureau until his name was finally cleared. He passed the test.

We need others to help us see our way past our flaws.

Take Friendly Fire

Effective leaders will learn how to accept constructive criticism when they need it. This is a test to pass. Sometimes we are blinded by sin in our own lives that blocks out the wisdom of God. We need others to help us see our way past our flaws. My friend Doug Winne, who is the pastor of the Evangelical Free Church in my community in Lititz, Pennsylvania, tells the story of how he faced this kind of friendly fire.

> As soon as I saw the deacon and the senior pastor walking
> to the door, I knew that something was up. I led them

into the living room and almost immediately heard these words, "Doug, we've come to talk to you about your critical spirit."

In the week prior to this visit, I received two independent calls, one from another pastor and the other from a friend. Both expressed concern over my "critical spirit." The first I had blown off as coming from a man who felt threatened by me; the second was harder to dismiss. Now two more men came and spoke to me about this same issue. I was crushed.

Almost immediately, I fell to my knees in front of these men. I wept as I cried out to God to forgive me and cleanse me of this sin. Some months later, my wife and I moved to Lancaster where I had the privilege of taking the role of a reconciler. Indeed, my life changed that day while on my knees; I went from always noting what was wrong to helping others find the good in one another. I had spent years noting people's faults; now I could spend years encouraging people in the grace of God in Christ.[1]

God will convict you if a criticism is valid. He desires for you, as a leader, to stay full of joy and the Holy Spirit, remaining flexible and creative as you mature and grow. So, in the long run, it helps to identify your blind spots. It gives you the opportunity to see yourself as others see you.

God will convict you if a criticism is valid.

Too many Christian leaders become cynical and sour from the challenges of leadership. The criticisms and obstacles they face as leaders make them bitter instead of better! They start to feel defensive and undervalued. But if leaders remain open to giving and receiving feedback, they become better at what they do, and God is glorified!

Find the Nugget of Truth

In his book *Axiom,* Bill Hybels talks of looking for the nugget of truth even in unhealthy and unfounded criticism we receive as leaders. It has been my experience that even when receiving criticism that is clearly loaded with false charges and nonsense, there is frequently an underlying element of truth that I need to deal with. I have three choices. I can simply disregard and throw out the entire criticism and never think of it again. I can dwell on it and rehash it and mentally defend myself time and time again. During this process I will mull over all of the reasons why the critic is an unwise and mean-spirited person.

I believe neither of these responses is best. The third response is to examine the criticism and discover the one percent or five percent of truth in the criticism and use it as an impetus for change and improvement as a leader. In this way, I can quickly forget the rest of the criticism and refuse to allow it to tear me down. I believe that the third response is the wisest as God develops leadership within me.

Become Offense Proof

There are some toxic attitudes that can paralyze and eventually destroy a leader's faith and leadership. One of these toxins is taking an offense. It's so easy to feel offended when something in which we feel strongly about is challenged or if a situation comes to a different conclusion than we had hoped for. What if we are trying to help someone and the individual, blinded by his own issues, lashes out at us? We tend to want to vent our feelings of frustration against that individual.

Offense is based on unforgiveness. Proverbs 18:19 says, *"An offended brother is more unyielding than a fortified city, and disputes are like the barred gates of a citadel"* (NIV). Taking offense allows the devil to build an "anti-God" stronghold around us based on unforgiveness. From that stronghold, the devil can attempt to cut us off from the Body of Christ and lead us into sin.

79

The Bible has much to say about taking an offense. Matthew 13:57 tells us that the people in Jesus' hometown were offended because of Him. Jesus said in Matthew 18:7 that offenses must come, but in Luke 7:23 He said, *"Blessed is he who is not offended because of Me"* (NKJV). In John 16:1 Jesus declared, *"These things I have spoken to you, that you should not be made to stumble* [be offended]*"* (NKJV). Proverbs 19:11 says, *"A man's wisdom gives him patience; it is to his glory to overlook an offense"* (NIV).

A biblical study relates the word *offense* to bait used to catch animals.[2] Monkeys are trapped by bait that is placed in a cage. When the monkeys reach into the cage to take the bait, they can escape only by releasing the bait and running away. But they usually do not want to release the prize, so they end up being trapped. If they would only release the bait, they could go free. When we forgive and release those who have offended us, we also can go free. It is up to us!

At various times in the Scriptures, prayer and forgiveness are coupled together (see Matt. 6:9-15; Mark 11:24-26). Forgiving others is crucial to maintaining a healthy, intimate relationship with Jesus. It is how we remain offense proof!

How to Handle Critics

The Bible tells us in Matthew 5:11-12:

> *God blesses you when people mock you and persecute you and lie about you and say all sorts of evil things against you because you are my followers. Be happy about it! Be very glad! For a great reward awaits you in heaven. And remember, the ancient prophets were persecuted in the same way.*

In his book *Confessions of a Pastor*, Craig Groeschel offers some advice on how to handle critics:

It's a fact that "hurt people hurt people." They usually dislike themselves and criticize others in a misguided effort to validate themselves. If one of these injured souls lobs a criticism grenade in your direction, defuse it with understanding. Part of considering the source is seeking awareness of what that person may be going through...

One time I was praying during worship, a few moments before preaching. Eyes closed, focusing on God, I felt someone slip a note into my hand. I never saw who it was, but the note was marked "Personal." I thought to myself, "Someone probably wrote a nice note to encourage me before I preach." A warm, loving feeling settled over me as I unfolded the paper.

A moment later, I lost that loving feeling.

Evidently, the note was from a woman who had tried to see me on Friday, my day off. She took offense at my absence and blasted me with hateful accusations. This happened literally seconds before I was to stand up to preach. In that moment, I had a choice. I could internalize the offense and become demoralized and discouraged. Or I could ask myself, I wonder what she's experiencing that caused her to lash out?

I chose compassion over depression. My heart hurt for her. I knew that such a disproportionate reaction must indicate deep pain, so I didn't take her note personally.

Consider the source. And consider the possibility that the jab may have come from an injured heart. Dismiss it and move on. If you don't, you may become the very thing you despise.[3]

Sometimes those in leadership feel like they are being criticized unjustly and they don't like it! And rightly so. The criticism may be totally unfounded. But when we receive correction or criticism, whether constructive or not, we must look to the cross. When we look at the cross, we look into the heart of God. We see our own need for cleansing and forgiveness and realize that although we may be rejected by others, we will never be rejected by God.

My friend Tim Brouse, who served as a youth pastor, tells a story of a time he experienced God's heart of love during a time criticism and rejection was heaped on him.

> I was playing quarterback on my high school football team as they battled for first place. My shot at becoming the beloved star of my community was in my grasp as I raced 60 yards toward the goal line. However, I zigged (I should have zagged), was tackled, and failed to score. We lost by one, and I lost my shot at hero status. My failure to succeed encouraged some fans to attack my character, vandalize my home, and even threaten my life. The windows of my home were covered with nasty names, and the insults dug deep into my heart. The next day, I woke up and there was no more graffiti, only windows washed clean. I ran to dad who said, "I didn't want you to have to see those names again; that's not who you are; you're my son and I'm proud of you." I wasn't shielded from the hurt but my father's actions demonstrated his love for me and pointed me to God.[4]

When we look to the cross, nothing else matters…there is love and mercy and truth. While it is true that "hurt people hurt people," it is also true that "healed people heal people."

—⚊—

In all the drama of false accusations and criticism, Tom did not try to defend himself. He drank the bitter cup without fighting back. Today,

God has given Tom a ministry far beyond the scope of what he had before. But like Jacob in the Bible, he walks with a limp. He will never be the same. He has a tender heart of compassion that is extended to everyone he meets. In looking back, Tom feels that the most valuable thing he learned was that his value is not in substance—how many people are in his ministry or how successful he appears as a leader. He learned that it is only in the presence of the Lord that he could find forgiveness for those who wronged him. Today he writes his life message that "mercy triumphs over judgment." His books have helped thousands who are facing the same betrayal that he has faced, and he gives them hope that the last chapter has not yet been written. God has turned it all around for good.

"If you do not forgive," he says, "you are the one who pays the price. Don't bad-mouth others or believe the worst. Sometimes your enemies will tell you things that you really need to hear that your friends will never tell you." He has passed the criticism test.

Endnotes

1. Doug Winne, "Crushed," *God Stories from Lancaster County* (Lancaster, PA: The Regional Church of Lancaster County, 2006), 369.

2. W. E. Vine, *Vine's Expository Dictionary of Old and New Testament Words* (Old Tappan, NJ: Fleming H. Revell Company, 1981), 129.

3. Craig Groeschel, *Confessions of a Pastor: Adventures in Dropping the Pose and Getting Real with God* (Sisters, OR: Multnomah Publishers, Inc., 2006), 169.

4. Tim Brouse, "Thanks Dad!" *God Stories from Lancaster County* (Lancaster, PA: The Regional Church of Lancaster County, 2006), 211.

The Criticism Test

Personal reflection questions/discussion

1. Why are false accusations the worst kind of criticism, and what should a leader's response be?

2. Think of a time when you experienced false accusations and how you responded to them. What did you learn about yourself? How would you change that response today?

3. What are some ways to offense proof yourself?

4. Describe a time you faced constructive criticism and how it affected you.

5. How does the Bible tell us to handle our critics?

6. How does forgiveness factor in when you are facing the criticism test?

—〜—

Chapter 8

The Dependency Test

An effective leader depends on help from God.

Pat, a single woman, was the missions director at a small midwestern church. She directed an exciting program of short-term missionaries traveling to countries throughout the world. She always encouraged anyone considering going on a missions' trip to trust God, *Jehovah-Jireh*, "God, our provider," for the finances. It was rare that anyone's needs were not met. She had witnessed the financial faithfulness of the Lord time and time again, not only for the missionaries, but for her own life as well.

One week Pat found herself in a situation where her meager ministry salary was running low. She was not worried. All her bills had been paid, and she had an adequate amount left over for groceries that week. Then she remembered. She had promised to travel to a neighboring city to participate at a soup kitchen that weekend, which was tomorrow! She needed funds for travel and lodging. Her grocery money was not enough. Her next paycheck was two weeks away. Her car was at the repair shop and would not be fixed until next week. "Okay, Lord, now what?" she prayed. Time was of the essence.

Yet Pat sensed that God wanted her to trust Him in this situation. She needed to practice what she preached and rely on Him to provide.

Early Saturday morning of the day of her expected travel, Pat awoke. She needed to be at her destination in three hours. She showered and packed her bag. She still didn't know how she would get to Chicago. She knew people were counting on her. She was starting to feel a little desperate. Why had she felt so strongly that God would provide? Maybe she had heard wrong. She should have called someone. She had many friends who would have been glad to help out. Was this a test? Would she pass? Pat fell to her knees in prayer.

—⟋⟍—

"My help comes from the Lord..." the psalmist declares in Psalm 121:2. He knew that God will allow us to be tested to see if our dependency is on Him or on our own abilities, money, or something else. Do we really believe that our help comes from the Lord and the Lord only? Do we stay dependent on the Lord day-by-day and minute-by-minute?

When we depend on the Lord we may or may not get the exact answers we were hoping for. But remember, He is God and we are not! We can't manage God or manipulate others to bring us the results we want or the way we wish them to be achieved. But when we depend on the Lord we realize that God is near and that He is our source. Then we know for sure that our help comes from the Lord.

God wants us to be desperate people. Desperate to know Him, that is! Philippians 3:8 says, *"Yes, everything else is worthless when compared with the infinite value of knowing Christ Jesus my Lord...."* Are you desperate to know more of God? Desperate leaders produce desperate people who want to know God—desperately!

Derrick was a lay elder in his church. As a businessman he had no training in pastoral ministry; however he had a close personal walk with God and a deep desire to be used by God. One day the senior pastor approached Derrick and asked him if he would consider delivering the message on a future Sunday when the senior pastor would be out of town. Although Derrick had never before preached a sermon, he immediately felt confirmation in his spirit that he should do it, so he quickly agreed.

The message he felt the Lord was asking him to deliver was on a potentially controversial topic. As he began preparation, several times he almost abandoned the topic entirely in favor of something much safer. However God continued to prompt him to stay with the original message. Additionally, Derrick felt like he should give an invitation at the end of the message, which further added to his discomfort. Finally Derrick decided that he would simply rely on the Holy Spirit and be obedient even though he knew that he was totally unequipped. He spent hours calling out to God and asking for His power and favor. The message went very well and was well received by the congregation. Many responded to the invitation. Derrick was so glad that he had put himself in a place where he had to depend on God rather than his own wisdom and strength. The results were so much better!

Dependency on the Lord and our personal prayer lives go hand-in-hand.

Daily Double

Dependency on the Lord and our personal prayer lives go hand-in-hand. We can tell how dependent we really are by checking out our personal prayer lives. In Luke 11:1-4 Jesus' disciples came to Him and said, *"Lord, teach us to pray...."* (Luke 11:1). In Matthew 6:6, Jesus said, *"When you pray, go away by yourself, shut the door behind you, and pray to your Father in private...."* In Matthew 26:41, Jesus instructed His disciples to *"Keep watch and pray, so that you will not give in to temptation. For the spirit is willing, but the body is weak!"*

Maintaining a healthy personal prayer life and having a complete dependency on the Lord is a constant test we face as leaders. In my book *Building Your Personal House of Prayer,* [1] I described a time when God convicted me that I needed to really learn how to pray. I was in Uzbekistan, meeting with leaders of the persecuted church. After our team of three Christian leaders taught from the Scriptures, they asked us questions. One question penetrated to my core. "Tell us about your personal prayer life," one of the Uzbek Christian leaders asked. "How much time do you spend with the Lord each day?"

I was suddenly uncomfortable and deeply convicted by God. I deferred the question to one of the other team members to avoid further embarrassment. I knew immediately I had been "weighed in the scales and found wanting." I left Uzbekistan with a deep conviction that I must learn to pray. I fervently believed in prayer, at least I thought I did. I taught on prayer, I went to all-night prayer meetings, I prayed daily, and I knew the importance of prayer in a Christian's life. I saw countless answers to prayer in my life and in the lives of others. But prayer seemed to be such a chore for me.

I needed help with my prayer life. I realized that if Jesus' disciples needed to request a model to help them pray, and Jesus suggested the Lord's Prayer, then this prayer was a clue to learning how to pray. Very soon the Lord gave me a fresh revelation of prayer that revolutionized my prayer life. I become conscious that He had called me to become a house of prayer (see Isa. 56:7). The Lord gave me a visual picture of a house with 12 rooms, each one corresponding to a part of the Lord's Prayer. As I enter each room, I learn 12 different ways to pray based on the model prayer of the Lord Jesus. My prayer life went from a duty to a joy! I became more aware of how completely I depended on the Lord each day.

Without a total reliance upon Him, all of our activities are doomed to failure. Warren Bennis in *Why Leaders Can't Lead* says that often the difference between success and failure, life and death, is the direction we're looking.

> The flying Wallendas are perhaps the world's greatest family of aerialists and tightrope walkers....I was struck with [Karl Wallenda's] capacity for concentration on the intention, the task, the decision. I was even more intrigued when, several months later, Wallenda fell to his death while walking a tightrope without a safety net between two

high-rise buildings in San Juan, Puerto Ricos....Later, Wallenda's wife said that before her husband had fallen, for the first time since she had known him, he had been concentrating on falling, instead of on walking the tightrope. He had personally supervised the attachment of the guide wires, which he had never done before.[2]

We can't afford to take our eyes off of Jesus. What does this kind of total dependency on the Lord look like? How can we trust Him in all aspects of our lives? In Psalm 127:1, King Solomon gives us good advice: Unless the Lord builds a house, the work of the builders is wasted.

Unless we are seeking the Lord in dependent worship and prayer on a regular basis, our work is wasted.

Unless we are seeking the Lord in dependent worship and prayer on a regular basis, our work is wasted. Only God alone can "build" and "watch over" our marriages, families, ministries, and businesses. The only way that we can truly reflect God's image is to develop a faith relationship with Him and with each other.

The Test of Dependency

Paul told the Corinthian believers,

> *But whatever I am now, it is all because God poured out His special favor on me—and not without results. For I have worked harder than any of the other apostles; yet it was not I but God who was working through me by His grace.* (1 Corinthians 15:10).

If our family seems to be doing well, it is not because we are such great parents. It is the grace of God! If our business or our church is growing and healthy, it is also because of the grace of God, not because of our leadership abilities. And if our business or our family or our church is in a season of struggle, it could be much worse, except for the grace of God.

In Philippians 3:10 Paul tells us, *"I want to know Christ and experience the mighty power that raised Him from the dead. I want to suffer with Him, sharing in His death."* Paul had passed the test. After all that he had accomplished as a leader in the New Testament Church, he was convinced that knowing Christ better was to be his main focus and ultimate desire.

Don't Fight the Current

It is our ministry in our families, churches, and workplaces to help each other stay close to Jesus and dependent on Him. Jesus wants first place in our lives because *"...He is first in everything"* (Col. 1:18). We must be desperate for the Lord. When we stay close to the Lord, we become more and more like Him. Are we desperate to know more of God? Desperate leaders produce desperate people who know it is all over if God does not show up.

A youth pastor at a local church in our area tells the story of a time he almost drowned when he tried to save a fellow swimmer. He was trained as a lifeguard and allowed his friend, a weak swimmer, to go out too far in the ocean thinking he could rest in his abilities as a swimmer. He recalls,

> We both got caught in a dangerous undertow. My friend began losing strength and panicking. Slipping out to sea, I began to fear for our lives as I tried to pull him in to shore. It seemed like a nightmare. No one was there to help us as we drifted further out! I seriously thought that this would be my last day on earth. Until I prayed with great desperation: "Lord Jesus, help us!" After praying, a thought struck me from the blue—"don't fight the current, swim sideways!" This was common sense, but I had forgotten it in the terror of the moment. I listened to that voice. Unbeknownst to us, within twenty feet was a sandbar. We soon stood in ankle-depth water hundreds of yards from the beach. We were safe![3]

As leaders, how many times are we like these two, trying to fight the current on our own, even to the point of exhaustion? Too often we make decisions without consulting the Holy Spirit. Many times, we act like we are independent rather than dependent on God. God's will is never to hurt or hold us down, but to give us the wonderful privilege of depending on the Lord. Are you in the midst of trouble in your life and fighting the current? Perhaps your deliverance is only twenty feet away. Are you ready to rest in God to lead you there?

—◊—

Pat was sure the Lord wanted her to participate at the soup kitchen for the weekend, but in this situation it seemed not only her money had run out, time had also run out. The doorbell rang. It was Pat's friend, Andrea. "What are you doing this weekend? I thought we could drive into the city and do something," she said. "I have some birthday money that's burning a hole in my pocket. The weekend's on me."

Pat grinned from ear to ear. "Do you want to help at the soup kitchen for a couple of hours today and tomorrow? After that, we can enjoy walking the Magnificent Mile and spending time at Millennium Park by the river."

This time Pat had passed the dependency test when it came to depending on the Lord for her finances. It was a lesson for her to realize that sometimes God withholds what we need until we're ready completely to rely upon Him instead of our resources. She knew that what she did with her money indicated what holds first place in her heart (see Matt. 6:21) and on whom she depends.

Endnotes

1. Larry Kreider, *Building Your Personal House of Prayer,* (Shippensburg, PA: Destiny Image Publishers, 2008).

2. Sermon Central, http://www.sermoncentral.com/SearchResults30 .asp. (Accessed March 2009).

3. John Wilkinson, "Fighting the Current," *God Stories from Lancaster County* (Lancaster, PA: The Regional Church of Lancaster County, 2006), 372.

The Dependency Test

Personal reflection questions/discussion

1. How is it possible to stay dependent on the Lord each day?

2. What happens when leaders start to depend on something or someone other than Jesus Christ?

3. Have you ever been caught up in the rat race of life and felt you were swimming against the current with no success? What did you do?

4. How does one make the transition from independence to dependence upon the Lord?

5. How do you know you are depending upon someone or something other than God?

—⁂—

Chapter 9

The Conflict Test

An effective leader embraces healthy confrontation.

North Shore Church was going through a crisis. There were harsh words spoken from the pulpit. There was resistance from the congregation. Both the leaders and the congregation were deeply hurt and angry. People were leaving in droves. Things seemed hopeless. As attendance and offerings dropped each week, everyone wondered if the congregation would survive. An ugly power struggle had emerged so the church leaders called in Sean, a leader from the congregation's denomination, to be a mediator.

The congregation favored the forced resignation of the pastor. The pastor blamed certain instigators in the congregation. There was a "blame game" going all around. Sean listened to both sides. At times, it seemed as though both the congregation and the pastor were intent on ruining each other entirely. As a leader, Sean knew that if the conflict was not settled soon, it would rip the church apart for good. How could he get them to see eye-to-eye again and offer grace and forgiveness to one another?

Without complete forgiveness, he knew that even after the dust settled, everyone's life could be adversely affected for years to come.

Could he help the North Shore Church congregation and its pastor to pass the conflict test?

—⁊⁊—

With a variety of people and their different ways of looking at situations, conflict is often inevitable.

You may have heard the story where a church deacon pulled out a gun and shot another deacon at a church leadership meeting. Obviously this is an extreme example, but the truth is that conflict does happen in our churches, families, and workplaces. People will disagree with one another and have differences of opinion. These conflicts may leave individuals feeling hurt, ignored, confused, isolated, or threatened. Unresolved conflict is compounded when people become stubborn and selfish and refuse to love biblically. It taints our ability to be productive, and we start blaming each other.

Conflict does not have to be unhealthy. It is a natural element of working together. Conflict is a test for us, often resulting from two different perspectives which derive from our different personalities, depending on how we are wired. Some of us welcome conflict and confrontation. Others run from it! If we accept conflict as a normal part of life, we probably struggle with understanding where others are coming from. We confront too quickly rather than trying to understand them.

If we hate conflict, we often fall into the "nice-guy syndrome." This causes us to make decisions that are more people-pleasing than God-pleasing. In our attempts to find acceptance from persons on both sides of a particular issue, we fail to be definitive enough, which confuses and frustrates others. In these situations, there seems to be an elephant in the room (an obvious truth that is being ignored or goes unaddressed) that we do not talk about, making us really dysfunctional. Whether we welcome conflict or try to avoid it, the lessons learned in the "conflict test" will help us to grow in life and in leadership.

Some time ago when I pastored our first church, one of the men in the church began to sow seeds of discontent. He was giving his opinion about how he differed with some of the decisions that the church leadership was making. It was done in a way that was not constructive. People were confused. His actions were also causing a strain on our relationship. When I realized what was happening, I faced my fears of confrontation and sat down with this brother and told him what I was seeing. He received my admonition, and today our relationship is restored.

As leaders, we need to be prepared to handle conflict because conflict will occur. Acknowledging this inevitability helps prepare us to do well in conflict. God tells us that we will have problems in this world (see Phil. 1:29). Unresolved conflict, however, will destroy teamwork.

Personality Conflict

Personality conflicts on a team can disrupt a team, causing frustration and a lack of cooperation. These natural sets of differences are some of our greatest strengths as individuals and teams; however, they are also sources of conflict.

Personality conflicts on a team can disrupt a team.

I believe every team should carry out some type of individual and team personality profile to understand how everyone's unique personality has been created in God's image. Understanding the diversity in personalities will help in understanding each other's strengths and weaknesses and will essentially help to avoid conflict.

When we are convinced that God has called each person as a member of our team, we are also convinced that each one has something unique to offer to the team. There can be no competition, because others' gifts and personalities bring wholeness to the team. When we understand others' strengths and weaknesses, we can build as a team, capitalizing on strengths and providing support where others are weak.

Allow Conflict to Be an Asset Not a Liability

I know several business leaders who have been trained by the "Sandler Sales Training" system. One of the key doctrines of this system is to, "seek first to understand, before you seek to be understood." Too many leaders approach a situation involving tension or conflict with a "fix" already in mind. However the parties involved seldom want to be "fixed." What they really want is someone to understand their position and to empathize with their plight. Many times leaders will discover that as they draw people out and genuinely seek to discover how they are feeling, the solutions will become obvious to all. Or at least their decisions will be more readily accepted because they are not imposing decisions on people who feel misunderstood and unappreciated.

The Bible gives us insight into resolving conflict. If handled biblically, conflict can become a real asset instead of a liability. Conflict often provides a time for teams to get to know each other better as individuals when they reveal their unique ways of thinking and feeling. Healthy working relationships will encourage the members to air their opinions freely and openly. Disagreements are an opportunity to demonstrate understanding, respect, and acceptance of others, thus strengthening relationships. Conflict allows us to recognize our deficiencies and invite the Lord to correct them as we grow spiritually.

Conflict allows us to recognize our deficiencies and invite the Lord to correct them as we grow spiritually.

Bill Hybels, pastor of Willow Creek Community Church in Illinois, admits that they expect conflicts on their church leadership teams.

The popular concept of unity is a fantasyland where disagreements never surface and contrary opinions are never stated with force. We expect disagreement, forceful disagreement. So instead of *unity*, we use the word *community*. The mark of community—true biblical unity—is not the absence of conflict. It's the presence of a reconciling spirit.[1]

Hybels gives the excellent advice of reminding leaders that they have a biblical responsibility "to take the high road of conflict resolution." The high road, of course, means conflict resolution according to God's Word. The first step is going directly to the person involved (see Matt. 18:15-17). Confronting and discussing the situation privately often gives an opportunity for quick resolution, lessening the chance for misunderstandings and animosity to grow.

Of course sin must be confronted if conflicts are to be resolved. Galatians 6:1-2 tells us:

Dear brothers and sisters, if another believer is overcome by some sin, you who are godly should gently and humbly help that person back onto the right path. And be careful not to fall into the same temptation yourself. Share each other's burdens, and in this way obey the law of Christ.

Sin (especially rebellion) divides and opens the door for more sin. Divisiveness is a sin. Leaders must be encouraged to focus on the nature and holiness of God. The fear of the Lord eliminates personal agendas and helps us to come into oneness in order to seek God's agenda.

Steps to Resolving Conflict

Let's look at some systematic principles to resolve conflict. Remember, conflict is not necessarily bad. Leaders are often strong personalities who have been successful in business or ministry and other areas of life because of boldly following what they believe is right.

Leaders on a team should learn to defer to each other. They must patiently learn to listen, forgive, receive, rebuke, correct, and submit to each other. But even with these patterns in place, conflicts will occur. Sometimes the conflicts are about a specific subject, and other times they may be about personalities and needs. James 4:1 reveals that our conflicts come from our desires. We want something different from what God desires. No matter what their origin, when conflicts occur, a leader's response should be to discern the reasons behind the conflict and the needs of those involved. The following principles apply to resolving conflict.

1. Gain Agreement That a Problem Exists

First, we must listen to each others' views on the subject at hand so it is clear as to what the conflict really is about. Define what issues are involved in the conflict and for whom it is a conflict. Pray for discernment to be able to detect any possible hidden issues in the disagreement.

In approaching the problem situation, we should begin by asking questions to draw the other(s) out. Statements tend to push people apart. Instead, ask questions. Try to understand the other's point of view. Try to find out what is behind each opinion. This helps another person see that you are willing to accept responsibility if you have contributed to the conflict.

Dialogue should use these kinds of phrases: "When you…I feel… because…" For example, "When you speak in that tone of voice, I feel like you are devaluing me because you are treating me like a child." This lets the other party know how you feel when the conflict is occurring.

Let the other person know how you react to the conflict. Listen for the feelings and emotions of the other and reflect on them with empathy and understanding. This creates an atmosphere of being cared for and listened to. It reduces defensiveness and focuses on the process involved rather than on the issues.

2. Identify the Consequences Up Front

Ask yourself, "What is the worst possible consequence if this conflict is never addressed and resolved?" One thing you should be able to agree on immediately is that if the conflict goes unresolved, it may lead to divisions on the team. This helps warn the group that the conflict should not be allowed to fester or remain unresolved.

Paul addressed dissension in the early Church by appealing for them to make an adjustment so that unity could prevail. He encouraged them to take immediate measures to repair their disagreements before strife tore them apart.

> *I appeal to you, dear brothers and sisters, by the authority of our Lord Jesus Christ, to live in harmony with each other. Let there be no divisions in the church. Rather, be of one mind, united in thought and purpose* (1 Corinthians 1:10).

When conflict is resolved, the team will reap the benefit of *"harmony with each other."*

3. Pray Together in Faith Asking the Lord for Wisdom and Solutions

Pray and ask the Lord to help you discern the reasons behind the conflict and what to do about it. *"If you need wisdom, ask our generous God, and He will give it to you...."* (James 1:5). Praying is a powerful way of seeking agreement. Sometimes the solution is revealed during the prayer time.

4. Mutually Agree on an Action

Too often we spend most of our time on the conflict and forget to pursue possible solutions. Make a list of any proposed action (solution). Then pray over the list and pick an action (possible solution) that everyone agrees with. Believe in faith for a win-win solution as you approach possible solutions together. *"Can two people walk together without agreeing on the direction"* (Amos 3:3). Will the proposed action allow a healing process to begin with no one being blamed? Does it provide for an end of the conflict with no recurrence? Will it result in better understanding by all parties with all feelings being respected? There is power in unity, and when we can agree on an action, the blessings of "life" the Lord promises in Psalm 133 will flow into the situation.

5. *Follow Up and Measure Progress*

Allow for a period of evaluation to determine if the resolution is successful in averting similar conflict(s). Set a specific date to meet and review the resolution and determine to alter the resolution if it is not working.

Once a conflict has been resolved and all the parties feel like they have been listened to, cared for, and understood, then it is time to "let go" of the conflict. The team and individuals involved should put the conflict behind them and forget it. Don't bring it up in the future. God does not remember our sins to hold them against us, and we should do the same.

6. *If the Conflict Cannot Be Resolved, Receive Help From an Objective, Trusted Outsider*

God is a God of restoration, and the goal of any conflict is always restoration. If a leadership team finds themselves at an impasse, an objective outsider, preferably a trusted spiritual advisor, can be brought in to help resolve the issue. Every person who has authority needs to be under authority. A conflict between leaders that cannot be resolved goes to the leaders who have appointed them and given them oversight. They have the God-given authority to bring resolution.

> *Obey your spiritual leaders, and do what they say. Their work is to watch over your souls, and they are accountable to God. Give them reason to do this with joy and not with sorrow. That would certainly not be for your benefit* (Hebrews 13:17).

Failure and Mistakes

The founder of Operation Mobilization, George Verwer, gives this sound advice to leaders having to deal with hurts and problems in the Church, "Get more familiar with the pain, and don't let it be such a big deal."[2] We are going to have pain. We are going to misunderstand and be misunderstood. We will be hurt at times. We will make mistakes. When we nurse our hurts and dwell on our mistakes, we allow ourselves to be hurt again and again. Although we must face the pain, we cannot dwell on it. Healthy leaders will forgive themselves and others so they can move on to the victory season of their lives. When we remain in the pain and the hurt, we will stunt our leadership growth. But when we face the pain and deal with the hurts, we will grow as leaders. It is our choice.

—⁓—

As a church leader in his denomination, Sean knew that to stave off conflict at North Shore Church, they needed extraordinary prayer. First he called for people to come together, not to discuss problems but to pray. But he also knew the church leaders must learn to develop certain skills. Sean soon realized that any communication is better than no communication so as he gathered the people together in prayer groups, he began to have discussion times. A wise leader, he listened and allowed them to share information that could help identify strengths and weaknesses. The people began to feel valued. He cautioned them to be careful with their conversation and only allowed conversation that aimed to seek to understand the other side and each other. They began to hear one another's hearts, not just empty words.

He encouraged the leadership and members to remain committed to follow Christ's teachings on love and on unity. Week after week, month after month, they prayed and they worked and they forgave each other. Gradually they learned to trust God and each other again. After many months they realized that they had not only survived but they became a healthy church that developed a good reputation as they served their community. Although it had been hazardous for their corporate spiritual health, in the end the test of conflict had helped them to grow. They will never be the same. They had passed the test.

Endnote

1.   *Building Church Leaders Notebook*, Theme 6: Handling Conflict, "Conflict Above Ground," an interview with Bill Hybels, (Christianity Today International).

2.   Anne & Ray Ortlund, *You Don't Have to Quit*, (Nashville, TN: Oliver Nelson, 1986), 61.

The Conflict Test

Personal reflection questions/discussion

1. Describe a time you engaged in healthy conflict with another. How about unhealthy conflict?

2. What is the nice-guy syndrome? How is this dysfunctional?

3. How does unresolved conflict destroy leaders and teams?

4. Describe how conflict can be resolved biblically.

5. Describe how you passed a test of conflict in your church, business, etc.

6. How can conflict help to grow and motivate us as Christians?

—ɯ—

Chapter 10

The Vision Test

*Effective leaders inspire and articulate a vision
and bring others with them.*

When Jane started her business she didn't even know how to spell *entrepreneur.* She only had a vision to own a tea shop. From a little girl on, she loved tea parties. In fact, she loved tea and all it entailed—scones with lemon curd and cream, mini-muffins, delicate cucumber sandwiches, fancy teacups and lacy tablecloths. She had a vision to provide a sanctuary for customers to enjoy their tea experience by using soothing colors, sounds, and materials. She knew exactly what her shop would look like because she had dreamed of it so often.

She envisioned the beauty, elegance, and charm of a Victorian tea shop where, in the time honored traditions of England, taking tea would be a time to reflect on the simple pleasures of life in the special company of dear friends and family. But the dream was not enough; within a year after starting, her first tea shop failed.

She was devastated and left wondering, "Why, God, did you give me this dream only to have it shatter?" Nevertheless, she picked up the pieces and studied a new business strategy. This time she was careful to create a business plan, get adequate start-up financing, and find strategic shop space for her new venture. She elicited the advice of other tea professionals to help develop her business. Now her vision and dream were being made a reality through sound strategy and the wise planning it needed to move ahead. But was all that enough? Was she communicating the vision clearly? Did she have good people to help her fulfill the vision? Her vision was facing the test.

—⚊—

There is no leadership without vision. In my travels, I find excitement in places where people have a vision. In California I met a man whose father migrated from Croatia and started a company in his garage—the Mag-lite Company. He had a vision. In Oshawa, Canada, I met a couple with a clear vision to reach the youth of their city. That ministry is now touching hundreds of youth. On the night I was there, 24 young people gave their lives to Christ.

Aluezio, my friend who lives in Goinonia, Brazil, had a vision 10 years ago to reach his city for Christ. Today there are 21,000 in his church, and many are helping him fulfill the God-given vision he has received for their city.

Just take a one-half hour drive from my home, and you will experience Hershey, Pennsylvania. Milton Hershey, the city's founder, had a vision for a company that would expand beyond the walls of his chocolate factory. He built homes, parks, schools, public transportation, and infrastructure, enriching the lives of those around him. His wealth was also accompanied by a profound sense of moral responsibility and benevolence. When he and his wife realized they could not have children, they founded a school for orphaned boys. In 1918, long before his death, Milton Hershey endowed the school with his entire fortune. He was a man with a vision, and today the name *Hershey* is a household name in many places and is a confectionery enjoyed by millions.[1]

The Bible is filled with examples of people who received a vision from God, and they changed the course of history: Abraham (a generous businessman), Jacob (a shrewd businessman), Joshua (a military officer), Moses (royalty in Pharaoh's household), Daniel (a government official), Amos (a farmer), Paul (a religious leader), Cornelius (an army officer), Peter (a fisherman). They inspired those around them as they communicated a vision of where they were heading and why it was important to head that way.

In the workplace or in the Church, people want to know that their work is adding up to a great cause. Most people want to make a difference in the world. They want to be inspired. Corporate companies know that the secret to inspiring people is to paint a picture of a world made better by their service or product:

> Think about it. Cisco CEO John Chambers doesn't sell routers and switches when he communicates to employees, colleagues, or customers—he sells a vision of an Internet that changes the way we "live, work, play, and learn." Starbucks founder Howard Schultz doesn't sell coffee beans—he sells the concept of a community, a "third place" between work and home. Suze Orman doesn't sell irrevocable trusts—she sells the vision of a life free of burdensome debt.[2]

Every good leader is driven by vision and should endeavor to pass it on to others. Former Secretary of State Colin Powell writes that a great leader should "find ways to reach down and touch everyone in a unit. Make individuals feel important and part of something larger than themselves."[3]

God wants to give His vision to every leader—something that is larger than themselves. My friend Sam Smucker who serves as pastor at the Worship Center in Leola, Pennsylvania, is a visionary leader who is influencing dozens of nations around the world. He says you have to be persuaded your vision is from God as you take steps to fulfill it.

**God wants to give His vision to every leader—
something that is larger than themselves.**

Vision is something from God in your spirit that gives you the ability to see beyond where you are now. Vision gives you a focus or something to reach for. Everybody ends up somewhere. Some people end up somewhere on purpose—the ones with vision! Without a vision, there is a lack of direction in our lives. It feels like we have no guidance woven through our lives. To have vision is to bring your world into focus.

When I was a farm boy, being able to see the end result gave meaning to otherwise boring work I had to do. For example, as I was plowing the field, I would picture my dad planting the corn. I would visualize the corn growing, being harvested, and taken to the barn to be made into feed for the cows. The cows produced milk, which provided food for people in the community.

Vision keeps the big picture in front of you. This picture will bring motivation and energy to the daily grind of vision coming to pass. For a vision to be realized there has to be faith in the vision. I call this the "faith factor"—being persuaded your vision is from God and taking steps toward it. The fulfillment of a vision is a process or a series of actions. The quality of our lives is determined by our vision and the effort we are willing to put into fulfilling it.[4]

The nature of vision is beyond reality. That's why it is called vision; it is forward thrusting, compelling, and pulling us into the future of what the Lord has for us. You must wait for it and take the time needed to formulate a clear mental portrait of where God is taking you. Even if it takes a long time for it to become a reality, patience waits until the timing is right. Impatience has resulted in the premature birth of many visions— before they are developed properly or fully.

Keep Your Focus

Walter was a fledging salesman. Following his training, his sales career began successfully. As a commissioned salesman, he enjoyed the freedom to arrange his own schedule. This was not a problem for Walter who was disciplined and dedicated to his job. After about a year on the job, Walter decided to leverage the flexibility of his new career and pursue his lifelong dream of obtaining his airplane pilot's license. He correctly reasoned that he could do all of his ground school and flying time early in the mornings when he was unable to make sales calls so it seemed it would not steal time from his new sales career.

However, that summer he found his sales dropping off sharply. At first he was uncertain what to attribute the decline in sales to. However, he soon came to realize that his focus had subtly changed. While the process of obtaining his pilot's license didn't steal precious time from his new sales career, he came to realize it had stolen something even more precious—his focus. Upon refocusing, his sales quickly picked up again.

Leadership is like selling in this regard, if our focus has been distracted, we will be ineffective and we will find ourselves floundering. This is why Paul the apostle said, *"I press on to reach the end of the race and receive the heavenly prize for which God, through Christ Jesus, is calling us"* (Phil. 3:14). I would say that Paul won the prize. And so can you and I if we keep our focus as Paul did.

Take a Vision Test

There are three stages to every vision—receiving it, the testing stage, and the fulfillment stage.

Receive the Vision

Every business, every ministry, every church, and every team needs a compelling vision. Our church's vision statement at DOVE Christian Fellowship International where I serve is, "To build a relationship with Jesus, with one another, and to reach the world from house to house, city to city, nation to nation." Vision articulated clearly and carefully will build trust among the people because it is something they can believe in. People will follow and embrace the vision as their own if they feel they are being led to a better future.

Did you ever try driving your car by looking at the line alongside the road? You will quickly find yourself off the road! To drive the car effectively, you have to look ahead—to where the car is heading. Vision is where the organization is going.

Proverbs 29:18 says, *"Where there is no vision, the people perish..."* (KJV). So unless your business or your church has a sense of direction and purpose, the people will probably struggle with a heart-felt connection to it. A relational heart-felt connection is important at all levels. Leaders can project vision, but if relationships of trust are not evidenced, vision will remain unfulfilled. If leaders are only interested in their personal vision being fulfilled by those within their realm of authority and responsibility, it will not be long until people feel used or taken advantage of. Wise leaders recognize that the process of sharing vision, building trust, and taking enough time for God's people to own the vision is as important as the vision itself.

If relationships of trust are not evidenced, vision will remain unfulfilled.

Prayer and vision go hand-in-hand. Prayer keeps us current with God's direction in our lives. Unity comes from praying together. Prayer is a powerful means of supporting each other and a spiritually bonding experience. This is one reason it is important for husbands and wives to pray together. Remember the disciples who were disputing about what position they would have in the Kingdom? They all dropped their desires for position and their ambitions in the prayer meeting in the Upper Room at the day of Pentecost. When a team comes together in prayer, it dissipates personal agendas and helps everyone focus on what God's agenda is for the team. Vision that is birthed in prayer is seldom second-guessed later.

Be open to new information. Stay open to learning new things and look for confirmation of the vision God has given you. A few years ago I read the book *The World Is Flat* by Thomas Friedman that explains the fast pace of globalization in our world today and the prevalence of outsourcing in our society. I now know why my Dell computer technical person is in Pakistan! I learned something new.

Test the Vision

Habakkuk 2:2-3 not only tells us to write a vision down but also says a vision may be tested. Big visions sometimes require big struggles to become a reality. God's purposes in the vision are moving ahead toward fulfillment, but there may be delays. What is God's timetable for the vision and how urgent is it? It was 12 years until Paul was asked to go to Antioch to teach. Moses missed God's timing by 40 years. Every team must seek the Lord to know how and when the vision will be fulfilled as they move forward to see it come to pass.

When waiting for a vision to be fully realized, the tendency is to try to figure out what is taking it so long. Our next tendency is to try and place blame on something or someone, "This vision is not becoming a reality because so and so is not praying enough or not pulling their weight." When team members begin to grumble against each other, the enemy can really come in with strife and division.

Every leader must check out his motivation. What in the vision is appealing to your ego? A young businessman told me, "I cannot wait to see a fleet of trucks with my name on it." It never happened. Maybe his ego got in the way. Deep in their hearts, effective and godly leaders must know this of their vision, "It's not all about me."

Are you prepared to pay the price? Be prepared for opposition. This is especially true if your vision has to do with invading the enemy's territory and setting captives free.

Implement the Vision

A leader should live with the vision for a season without moving too quickly. Pray for wisdom about the details for the vision. The One who gave you the vision will be the One to provide the means to accomplish it in every detail. Vision is conceptual; we must make it practical. The vision must always come down to an achievable project. In Nehemiah's case, it was to build a wall. David received a vision to build the temple, but God said Solomon would actually be the one to accomplish it.

Vision is always about the future. It is about something not yet achieved or experienced. It is the stretching of reality beyond anything you are currently experiencing. My wife LaVerne and I had a vision at the start of our marriage for a healthy marriage, so we started having date nights to keep our relationship exciting and alive. We are still enjoying those dates 38 years later. What we implemented worked!

If the vision is to be realized, it must be shared and owned by others. Most visions cannot be fulfilled by one person. God builds teams. Most believers find direction for their lives by embracing a vision that God has given to someone else. In the end, it matters little who received the original vision. When we embrace a vision, the vision belongs to all of us.

Recruit others to help. Leaders must know how to take people with them through the process of fulfilling a vision, and they must know how to help others fulfill the vision the Lord has given to them. The Bible tells us in Habakkuk chapter 2 that we should write the vision down on tablets so we can run. There is something about writing the vision down that helps us to formulate it clearly in our minds. It also helps us to not forget our God-given vision. And when it is written down, our "vision statement" becomes a tool to clearly communicate the vision to others so that the vision can be fulfilled together by a team of people.

—⚋—

Today, Jane is the owner of 12 specialty tea shops. Her vision had not only survived, it prospered and expanded! The 16-hour workdays and wise decision making on her part helped turn it into a success with revenue to prove it. She wrote her vision down and surrounded herself with staff that joined her in her vision and also wanted to see it succeed. Jane realized it was not enough just to receive a vision from the Lord; she also had to learn how to communicate it properly and invite others to join with her to help accomplish it. Only then would her God-given vision be fulfilled.

Endnotes

1. "About Milton S. Hershey," *The Hershey Story,* http://www.hersheystory.org/about/milton-hershey.aspx (accessed April 2, 2009).

2. Carmine Gallo, "The Secret of Inspiration," *BusinessWeek* (June 1, 2005), http://www.businessweek.com/smallbiz/content/jun2005/sb2005061_7854_sb037.htm (accessed April 2, 2009).

3. Colin L. Powell, *My American Journey* (New York: Random House, 1995), 58.

4. Sam Smucker "The Faith Factor," *God Stories from Lancaster County* (Lancaster, PA: The Regional Church of Lancaster County, 2006), 104.

The Vision Test

Personal reflection questions/discussion

1. Do you have a vision as a leader? How do you bring others alongside your vision?

2. Why is it important for people to have a heartfelt connection with the vision of the leader?

3. How do prayer and vision go hand-in-hand?

4. Describe a time your vision was tested.

5. How can ego get in the way of vision?

6. As a leader, you will come across those who do not think in terms of "writing down the vision." How will you help them grow in developing vision?

—⚍—

Chapter 11

The Love Test

*An effective leader makes decisions motivated
by love.*

Kimberly led a women's Bible study group at Good Shepherd Church which met in the church basement every Thursday evening. An inner-city church, Good Shepherd was intent on reaching out to the many low-income people in their neighborhood. Kimberly was a seasoned church leader and social worker and accustomed to the unique issues facing women in her city. But she had never experienced a person quite like Alexa, a single mom who, with her two children, started attending Kimberly's Bible study group. Alexa had led a complicated life—childhood trauma, poor decisions, drug use, and failed relationships.

But Alexa had recently come to follow Jesus. She had an unswerving faith and trusted the Lord for every situation that came up in her life.

She soon shared her dreams with the group of becoming a part-time teacher's assistant and working with disabled children. Only trouble was—Alexa had a fourth grade reading level. She had never finished high school. She was currently on public assistance. The odds were stacked against her.

When Alexa asked Kimberly to help her study for her high school equivalency test, Kimberly's first inclination was to say no. Her schedule was maxed out as it was. And really, Alexa just didn't seem to have the mental capacity to do it. And if she was honest, Kimberly didn't want to waste her precious time in an endeavor that would most likely get her nowhere. When it came right down to it, the whole idea just seemed like a time drain on Kimberly's already busy schedule.

On the other hand, would she practice what she preached? Just last week the Bible study lesson was about unconditional love and about giving with no expectancy of return. Was this a test for her as a leader?

—⚏—

Most leaders are familiar with the love chapter in the Bible. The Greek word for love in this chapter is *agape*, a love which gives *with no expectation of return*. The *agape* love test for leaders is often our temptation to favor certain people because of their influence or for what they can do for us. One church leader repented after he realized he was favoring a wealthy church member who owned a yacht, and his underlying motivation was to spend time on the yacht! We must constantly be aware of showing partiality. Everyone, great and small, is precious in God's sight.

> **The *agape* love test for leaders is often our temptation to favor certain people.**

Agape love is the straight arrow of love that flies free in one direction to give to others unselfishly. John 3:16 speaks of this love, *"For God so loved..."* We can be sure that a leader's love will be tested to see if it is unconditional. Our Savior was compassionate about people and their needs. When Jesus saw the crowds, He had compassion (see Matt. 9:36). Compassion compels us to give and not be upset if something is not given back to us. Colossians

3:12 tells us to clothe ourselves with compassion. Compassion, unlike pity, gives people a path out of their pain. A pastor tells this story about passing the test of love for someone who was difficult and hard to love.

> As a teenager, I helped tend a produce market stand. One of our regular customers was a middle-aged woman who bought a few tomatoes every week. She became my "enemy" as each week I listened to her complain while she aggressively sorted through the pile of home-grown tomatoes, squeezing each one firmly enough to bruise.
>
> One Saturday, my "tomato enemy" once again began sorting through the beautiful quantity of tomatoes. I waited on her grudgingly, fuming as I watched her deliberately squeeze each one. My attitude wasn't helped as I witnessed her steal two tomatoes, dropping them into her basket. Needless to say, I was angry, but I finally had the opportunity for vengeance!
>
> I quickly informed the owner. I wasn't prepared for his reply. He instructed me to get a large paper sack, fill it with the nicest tomatoes, and give them to her freely. "Tell her she doesn't need to steal any of them. If she can't pay, we will gladly supply her, free of charge, all the tomatoes she needs," he said.
>
> I did what I was told, and that act of love did something for us both; it changed our hearts. In the ensuing weeks I developed a strange friendship with my new "friend" as I learned to know her name and that she was a single mom struggling to raise a handicapped son.[1]

Love at a Whole New Level

God expects a Christian leader, serving both in the church and in the workplace, to love others with an unconditional love. When Jesus walked with His disciples on this earth, He taught them the Golden Rule—*"Do to others whatever you would like them to do to you..."* (Matt. 7:12). However, just before He left, He told them He was giving a new commandment.

> *So now I am giving you a new commandment: Love each other. Just as I have loved you, you should love each other. Your love for one another will prove to the world that you are My disciples.* (John 13:34-35)

Jesus' new commandment was to "love each other as I have loved you." The new commandment challenges and moves us far beyond the old commandment of loving others like we want to be loved. Now we are commanded to treat others as Christ has loved and treated us. This takes us to a whole new level. It moves us beyond our personal preferences and causes us to esteem others as more important than ourselves. At this point, the focus is not what is important for me; it is what is best for my team (or followers). How can my team advance into the greater things of God? God expects leaders to nurture and care for their followers. A Jesus-style of leadership is loving and is focused on the needs of others.

With the old commandment, you are still the center of your universe, and everything depends on *your* human capacity to love. When you move away from being the center of your universe, you are challenged to love unconditionally like Jesus loves. A leader will unselfishly place others first (see Phil. 2:2-7).

A leader will unselfishly place others first.

A true leader's main goal is not to preserve life or position; it is to advance the Kingdom of God. It is not the building of our business or our own ministry that should consume us; it is advancing God's Kingdom. While speaking on the topic of "passion," my friend, Floyd McClung, has said: "I can tell when I have lost my passion for Jesus when I make decisions based upon what it will cost me versus the glory that Christ will receive."

A friend of mine has been elected to a local school board. He is often confronted with the dilemma of making the right decision for the school district, knowing that he will be criticized by the press for doing it. Often in leadership you are misunderstood because you have information that can't be shared publicly. There is nothing you can do about it—you will be misunderstood. Leaders do not always have to explain themselves. It is OK to be misunderstood.

Love, Loyalty, and Faithfulness

The combination of these three character traits is powerful. Some people are one or the other, and that spells trouble. A dog may be your most loyal friend and faithfully greet you as you enter your home after a day at work. But if he responds to everyone with that same loyalty, he will allow a burglar to come in your house and take everything you have! A dog like this is loyal, but not faithful.

A team member can faithfully show up at every meeting and event of the church, but if he is not loyal enough to jump into the fray when spiritual battles need to be fought in the church, he will allow satan to tamper with God's people and his leader. Leadership teams stand together in both loyalty and faithfulness and love. Strong churches are made up of a group of people who genuinely love each other and those they serve, who loyally fight together against the spiritual enemy who is trying to destroy them. They do not fight with each other!

There is a story from the Vietnam War that tells of a platoon coming under a surprise attack. They fell back to a safe zone, but one of the men was wounded and lying out in the open field. His friend told the commanding officer, "I must get my friend."

The officer said, "I absolutely forbid you to run out there; it is too dangerous." But the young private ran off into the field, amidst the fire and explosions, to pull his best friend to safety. He arrived back to the safe zone with his friend, and the officer looked down at the man, now dead. He asked, "Well, private, was it really worth it?"

The young man, with tears in his eyes, responded, "Yes sir, it was. The last words he spoke to me were, 'I knew you would come.'"

This is the kind of unconditional love God wants us to have. The enemy will attack. Can we remain steadfast and loyal and love others unconditionally when the pressure is on?

—⁓—

Kimberly took the matter to the Lord in prayer. The Lord spoke to her spirit, "I love Alexa with an unconditional love, and I want you to do the same." It was enough for Kimberly. She started to tutor Alexa every week. For weeks and weeks it seemed as if they made no headway, but then a light-bulb seemed to go on in Alexa's head. Words started to make sense, her school lessons became easier. Eventually, she passed her high school equivalency exam and achieved her dream of working part-time as a teacher's assistant with a disabled child in a local school.

"What if I had said 'no' to Alexa?" Kimberly thought. "Lord, forgive me. It's so easy to love those who are good-looking, smart, or fun to be around. But when people inconvenience me or I feel I will not get anything back in return, it's easy to turn away. Help me to reach out and be a true example of *agape* love. Help all my relationships to be about love without conditions."

Endnote

1. Wesley D. Siechrist, "Kind Words," *God Stories from Lancaster County* (Lancaster, PA: The Regional Church of Lancaster County, 2006), 297.

The Love Test

Personal reflection questions/discussion

1. How can a leader's heart go beyond the Golden Rule of "doing unto others as you would have them do unto you" and move into agape love?

2. How has your love been tested to see if it was unconditional?

3. Have you ever been tempted to favor someone because of what they can do for you? How?

4. How do love, loyalty, and faithfulness go hand-in-hand?

5. If God is love and we are made in His image, what inhibits us from loving as He loves?

—⚍—

Chapter 12

The Integrity Test

*Effective leaders are the same in public
as in private.*

When missionaries, John and his wife Sharon, were preparing to move to South America for missionary service, the organization for which they would work in Brazil asked them to bring several thousand dollars worth of sophisticated audio/video equipment along. In order to save the high import tax on such items, they asked John and Sharon to include the equipment as part of their personal household belongings. These were exempt from customs fees. John and Sharon were in a dilemma. They felt this would be a misrepresentation, so they respectfully told their employer that they would gladly bring the items, but they would not say that they belonged to them.

The mission agency was frustrated, believing that John and Sharon would cost them many hundreds of dollars in customs duties. Nevertheless, John and Sharon stood their ground. They believed that God would honor truthfulness. They flew to Brazil and were soon notified that their freight was at the airport for pick-up. Along with two men from the mission and a borrowed truck, John went to claim the items.

The customs officers looked over the list John had prepared. Each household item was listed and each expensive AV item was clearly marked as not belonging to him personally, but rather to the mission. Immediately he asked to see each one of these items. John opened the freight containers and pointed out each item. John couldn't help but think, *I wonder if it is going to be worth it to be totally honest?* But it didn't matter really, because this was a test of integrity and he was intent on passing it!

Three young ministers of the Gospel were bursting onto the ministry scene in the late 1940s. Two of the three had already achieved notable influence. Chuck Templeton and Bron Clifford were preaching dynamos. One university president, after hearing Templeton preach to a crowd of several thousand, called him the most talented and gifted young preacher in the United States. Bron Clifford was also believed to be someone who would greatly impact the Church world. Both Templeton and Clifford started out strong. But by 1950, Templeton left the ministry in pursuit of a career as a radio and television commentator. He eventually decided that he no longer believed in orthodox Christianity. Clifford's story is nothing short of tragic. By 1954, he had left his wife and two children. Alcohol was the vice that destroyed his life. Only nine years after being the most sought-after preacher in the United States, Clifford was found dead in a sleazy motel room.[1]

You may be wondering who the third evangelist was. His name is Billy Graham. While Templeton and Clifford were enjoying their success, Graham was establishing boundaries within his personal life and ministry that would ensure his longevity. He has been a leader that has led with integrity for many, many years.

A leader who "has integrity" is honest and has clear and uncompromised values and clarity about what's right and wrong. *Integrity* comes from the same Latin root as *integer*. You may remember integers from math—they are whole numbers. *Integrity* means "whole or complete."

A leader who leads with integrity is leading completely.

When we live in right relationship and open communication with God, it brings our lives to wholeness. We are living with integrity from the inside out. We are not trying to conceal parts of ourselves from God, from others, or from even ourselves. A leader who leads with integrity is leading completely.

Titus 2:7-8 tells us:

> ...*Let everything you do reflect the integrity and seriousness of your teaching. Teach the truth so that your teaching can't be criticized. Then those who oppose us will be ashamed and have nothing bad to say about us.*

Integrity means we are completely open about our lives, hiding nothing.

In our church's publications department, our staff makes every effort to walk in integrity when working with vendors to complete our printing projects. So many things can go wrong, and it often takes patience to work through discrepancies. We endeavor to remain gracious in our dealings with the vendors and try to give adequate time for them to complete the project rather than demanding a quick turnover. Integrity means we treat sales representatives with respect and kindness so we cannot be criticized for bad behavior.

Barriers to Integrity

On the opposite spectrum, when integrity is absent, leaders lead from a vacuum created when trust is lost. Newspapers are full of stories of people who demonstrate little integrity in their dealings with others, like the business leaders of Enron and WorldCom who damaged others' livelihoods and well being by their lack of integrity and greed.

When integrity is absent, leaders lead from a vacuum created when trust is lost.

As a Christian leader, you must align your attitudes, words, and actions with biblical truth. If you want to finish well with your integrity intact, you have to be aware of the things that are barriers to integrity, such as the misuse of money, the abuse of power, the pride of success in ministry, sexual misconduct, family dissention, complacency, and the list continues. All these issues are deeply rooted in character issues and personal integrity. If there is a crack in your character, one day it will be opened. It really does start with the little things. First Thessalonians 5:22 tells us to *"Stay away from every kind of evil."* This means we must walk in complete purity. Sometimes it is the little decisions we make that prevent us from making big mistakes. A local ministry leader tells this story of an example of integrity from his dad's life.

During the 1930's Depression, my father moved to a cheap one-room apartment in Chicago in the hopes of finding work. He spent most of his days on his feet, walking from business to business, applying at every place he could find.

Across the hall from dad's room was a man named Al. Al seemed to always be throwing parties. He took a liking to my father and offered my dad a high paying job—to stand on a certain street corner at a certain time, passing on a package to one of Al's customers.

My dad thought about it for a long time and decided that he did not want to get involved. He was not sure why—he just did not have a good feeling about it. Al tried to convince my dad to take it. He put his arm on my dad's shoulder and said, "C'mon Vernie, it's good money, and I know you won't find such an easy job like this anywhere else! Besides, I know you are hungry and could use a good job."

My dad thanked Al, but told him that it just did not seem right to accept it. Al gave an "okay, no hard feelings" kind of a response, and they went their separate ways. Eventually, dad did get a job in which he could support himself and forgot about the incident. Years later, as he picked up a copy of a newspaper with a picture of his friend, Al, and the headlines "Al Capone, Gangster, Dead," he was especially glad that he did not take the job that "good ol' Al" offered him![2]

My friend and colleague, Ron, was influenced by a time he witnessed his father-in-law passing the test of integrity. As a young man, Ron, his father-in-law, and two brothers-in-law owned one of the largest farms in their county. They were well-known by the equipment dealers because they wanted their business. One particular time, Ron's father-in-law gathered quotes from local dealers to buy three high horsepower tractors. A decision was made, and he verbally told one dealer that he would purchase from him. A few hours later, another dealer dropped by and offered the tractors at a much more discounted price. Ron's dad would save hundreds of dollars.

Ron never forgot what his father-in-law said. "We can save a lot of money by buying the tractors from this company, but we gave our word that we would purchase them from the first dealer, so we will be men of our word and buy them from him." It had a profound impact on Ron's life. He learned that an honorable man keeps his commitments and follows through on his obligations. In doing so, he passes the integrity test!

Checks and Balances Needed

Every Christian believer is well aware of the realities of the deceitfulness of sin that starts with making one bad choice or decision. This should cause us to desire accountability in our lives. Everyone needs practical accountability, including Church leaders. Christian leaders need to be accountable to others for the way they live their Christian lives and for the way they are directing churches, ministries, and businesses. As leaders, we need to have checks and balances—accountability—in all levels in our lives because we will be tested in the area of integrity.

For example, since pastors are those chosen and appointed to oversee the church, their lives are known to the people in the church. They live their lives in full view of others, and this is extremely healthy. When a leader is "real" he helps others be transparent too so they can help each other. With these close relationships, they have a built-in accountability surrounding them.

Athletes who train together push each other to greater heights. The same is true in leadership teams as leaders sharpen and encourage each other in every area of life. A team of leaders working together in close relationship provides a structure for genuine accountability. It is hard to hide sins of pride, greed, or the love of power when the surrounding team provides built-in accountability. The peer relationships of leaders who are open with their lives serve to help each other in weaknesses and nudge each other to accomplish their responsibilities before the Lord. Wise leaders will welcome accountability and choose to walk in purity and accountability in full view of those they lead.

Satan Targets Leaders

Pastors and other visible leaders of the Church are examples to the rest of the Church, but they are not immune to temptations. Adam and Eve, David and Bathsheba—the failures of Bible greats are on public display to attest to the fact that leaders are as susceptible as anyone. Satan is out to steal, kill, and destroy, and he will target leaders because he knows "the bigger they are, the harder they fall." In other words, the ministry of a leader touches a great number of people, so if he is tempted and succumbs to sin, the repercussions are often more heartbreaking and far-reaching.

With leadership and its responsibilities and potential stressors, there are three major temptations that can lurk, waiting to derail a Christian leader's ministry and integrity before God. First John 2:16 lists these three temptations as sexual temptation (the cravings of sinful man), the love of money (the lust of the eyes), and pride (the boasting of what he has and does).

Notice that these three are twisted versions of legitimate and wonderful gifts God wants to give us. Sex, within its perimeters of marriage, is a wonderful gift. But the emphasis of sex outside of marriage in today's sex-saturated society makes it a challenge to stay morally pure, bringing great devastation to those who succumb. As a young leader I learned that Billy Graham set a standard in this area, and I chose to follow his example. He would not spend time alone with a woman other than his wife or daughters. He has been committed to "abstaining from every appearance of evil," and Billy is finishing well. He has passed the test!

God blesses us with money to advance His Kingdom here on earth and provide for our needs. On the other hand, *the love of money* turns some away from serving the Lord faithfully. If Jesus is not Lord of a leader's money, He will not be Lord of his life. Jesus did not manipulate the message of the Kingdom for personal gain. When the rich young ruler expressed interest in the ministry of Jesus, the disciples probably were thrilled. With his great wealth, he could easily take care of their financial needs. But Jesus told him to sell everything and give the money to the poor and follow Him. Jesus did not ask for anything for Himself. He would not compromise His integrity (see Luke 18:18-25).

If we trust in our accomplishments, it leads to pride. A leader is often a self-motivated person and willing to step in where others are hesitant. This drive, which may direct the leader to great success, can negatively lead him to pride. A pastor with a thriving church, for example, needs to guard his heart to avoid the temptation of becoming puffed up with pride.

All of us have a desire to be productive and fruitful. However, if our desire to bear fruit pushes us to cut corners, ultimately all the fruit will be lost. Proverbs 2:7 says we will be protected by our integrity because the Lord will be *"a shield to those who walk with integrity."*

Integrity is a critical component to inspiring trust in leadership. When a leader's character is marked by integrity, people will follow. A leader who leads with integrity is leading completely.

—⁓—

Remember John and the video equipment he declared at customs rather than misrepresenting it as his own belongings? Here's the rest of the story:

The customs official looked at the items and walked away. A few minutes later he returned and told John to load up all the containers and leave. There would be no import tax, no request for a bribe (a common practice), no problems. A process that typically took several days was completed in less than an hour!

John was humbled and amazed at God's goodness and challenged again to obey His instructions, even when they might seem foolish. He had passed the integrity test!

Endnotes

1. Steve Farrar, *Finishing Strong* (Sisters, OR: Multnomah Books, 1995), 4-5.

2. Jim Schneck, "Integrity," *God Stories from Lancaster County* (Lancaster, PA: The Regional Church of Lancaster County, 2006), 12.

The Integrity Test

Personal reflection questions/discussion

1. For me as a leader, not to walk in integrity would mean....

2. Make a list of some of the "inside" and some of the "outside" boundaries necessary to maintain integrity.

3. How does integrity cause me to lead in a "complete" manner?

4. Name some barriers to integrity.

5. What areas of my life do I need more transparency and a greater level of accountability to finish my life well?

—◊—

Chapter 13

The Security Test

Effective leaders find security in who they are, not in what they do.

Chris was a township supervisor who struggled with his own sense of worth. His position of authority in his community gave him a sense of significance. He felt important because he was the first official contacted about any township business, he moderated township meetings, and he was perceived as the township spokesperson. But with this authority he was also the first person to be contacted when there were any township complaints. Chris got plenty of those!

Lately he was criticized for moving ahead on a large inter-municipal project that many citizens in his township opposed. The straw that broke the camel's back happened when he was accused of overspending public money in his decision to replace all the aging streetlights in the township. Chris became depressed and angry at the same time. He had done so much for the people in his community. *Hadn't the township been awarded a one million dollar federal community development block grant that would greatly benefit the community? Hadn't he acquired an excellent five-year trash-hauling contract for his township? Maybe he just didn't have what it took to be a leader. Why had God led him to this position only to have it humiliate him and make him look incompetent?* His role in representing the township's communal interests seemed to be going down the tubes. Would Chris find his security in the Lord and learn how to react to the reactions of others in a healthy way? Would he pass the test?

—⁊⁊⁊—

Most people feel insecure in one way or another. I have felt misunderstood, left out, and rejected many times in my life. In my first year at school, I was one of those kids who was usually the last one picked to play baseball with my schoolmates. It really hurt. I developed insecurities in my emotional makeup that I had to allow Jesus to touch. When I finally realized that "Jesus loves me this I know, for the Bible tells me so," it was the greatest truth I ever learned. I could be secure in the fact that God loved me. Jesus accepted me just the way I was. I could accept others because I now knew that God completely accepted me!

Unlike Chris the township supervisor, Jesus knew who He was. He did not react to the reactions of others because He had a fear of being discovered as unsuited to meet His responsibilities. Jesus knew who He was, where He came from, and where He was going, according to John 8:14. He was secure in His Father's love. That's why He could kneel down and wash His disciples' feet in the Upper Room, even when He knew what would soon happen. He took upon Himself the role of a servant because He was safe and secure that His Father would be there, on the other side of death, to raise Him up again.

Leaders do not need their egos stroked in order to function in their role as leaders.

Leaders who are secure in their heavenly Father's love are free to serve, expecting nothing in return. They do not need their egos stroked in order to function in their role as leaders. They have a healthy belief in themselves and do not look to others for acceptance and approval. They are happy to serve because they know they are deeply loved by God.

Facing the Insecurities

Healthy leaders will deal with their insecurities so they are not paralyzed by them. Nobody is confident all the time in all situations. As a leader, you may sometimes feel as though you are not "good enough." It seems as if everyone else looks so good, so together; and you feel out of it compared to them. I remember my insecurities as a young pastor sometimes overpowered me when I invited a guest speaker to speak at our church. Afterward, members of the congregation raved about his message and how it helped them. I knew that I had used the same Scriptures and spoken a similar message just a few weeks earlier, and I had not gotten such an enthusiastic response! I really had to let go of the inadequate feelings. I was too critical of myself and it was not easy for me to believe others were not also as critical. I was facing a test of security. I had to break through the barrier of the self-doubt and move on.

John C. Maxwell, an internationally recognized leadership expert, says there are "few things worse than an insecure leader." He backs it up with a list of characteristics that insecure leaders have in common that make them so ineffective.

> **They want control.** Control is everything to insecure people; the thought of giving it up by empowering others or delegating important responsibilities scares them to death.

> **They fear public failure.** As a result, they will absolutely do anything to avoid being embarrassed by doing something stupid in front of others.

They avoid risk. They would rather not try and not know, even if it means missing out on great success and growth.

They are closed in their relationships. They don't open up because they fear rejection.

They do not hire 10s. If they did, they'd run the risk of being shown up. So instead of hiring top-notch people, they surround themselves with mediocrity.

They resist change. Keeping the status quo helps them maintain control, or so they think.

They fail to affirm and empower others. Many insecure people weren't affirmed or empowered during critical phases of life. As a result, they're practically incapable of nurturing the people they lead.

They stay in their comfort zone. To leave it invites risk and change—what more can I say?

They view people and situations through their insecurities. Consequently, what they see never totally matches up with reality, and more often than not, it's completely skewed.

They create an environment of insecurity. This makes the people they lead confused and unsettled because they never know what's going to happen next.[2]

Then Maxwell gives us some good news. If we identified with some or all of the characteristics in this list, there is hope. We recognized there is a problem, and now we must take the steps toward overcoming it. Here are his four suggestions:

Seek professional help. Find a good counselor, and figure out a way to get off the roller coaster of personal insecurity. You owe it to yourself, the people you lead, and the people you love.

Identify your areas of insecurity. The counselor will help you do this, and he or she will also give you practical ways to overcome your insecurities.

Allow a trusted friend to help you. This will mean opening up about your deepest insecurities, but it's always easier to battle this kind of problem with a supportive friend than it is to do it alone.

Develop a complementary friend. If your trusted friend also complements your insecurities and helps make up for some of your weaknesses, you'll be well on your way to overcoming this problem.

It won't happen overnight, but when you finally learn to deal with or even eliminate your personal insecurities, you'll be amazed at the difference it makes in your life and in the lives of the people you lead.[3]

The Bible tells us in First John 2:27 that we *have an anointing* from the Lord within us. When we are secure in that anointing as leaders, we can empower others.

Henry Ford had an incredible vision. The car he manufactured changed modern life. And yet, he was so personally insecure that he could not keep himself from undermining the other executives at the Ford Motor Company. He would empower subordinates only to cripple their authority later. Worries about job security usually prevent leaders from empowering other people, but the ability to develop other leaders makes you invaluable to your organization. Abraham Lincoln named his political rivals and critics to his cabinet because he wanted the benefit of advice from leaders as strong or stronger than he was. When you empower others, you lift them up and, in the process, you elevate yourself.[4]

A Security Test

How you react to those who rebel against your authority as a leader—whether it is your kids, employees, team members, or church members—will tell how secure you are as a leader. Aaron and Miriam criticized Moses regarding the leadership decisions that He was making. They were jealous of Moses and did not fear God or respect God's prophet. This allowed a spirit of rebellion to come into their lives. Moses was secure enough as a leader to react in kindness to their act of rebellion. He did not defend himself. Instead he went to God, and God defended him. What's more, Moses implored God to remove the punishment of leprosy from Miriam. This was a test that Moses passed.

Insecure leaders often want and need control.

Insecure leaders often want and need control. Feeling insecure, they search for and seek out opportunities to make themselves look important. Their ego is their driving force. Because they do not feel secure in the vision and direction they are going, they start to push and make something happen to somehow "save face" for their identity and reputation.

God did not design a ministry for our own needs to be met, but to help meet the needs of others. If we use a ministry that God has given to us in the Church, workplace, or in our families for a purpose that God did not intend it to be used for, we become blinded by our insecurities. We become dysfunctional.

The reality of leading others is that mistakes will be made, but leaders who are secure in Christ realize that failure is only an event, not who they are. The Lord helps every leader survive the ups and downs of leadership with its challenges. As he serves others, a secure leader is secure in who he is. His goal is to allow God to satisfy his heart and to care less about what others say about him.

Chris's insecurity as a leader finally brought him to a point of brokenness. Through counsel from a wise mentor, Chris was able to discern his true source of security in God's love for him as a Christian man and as a leader. He began to recognize that he would not please everyone in his leadership position as a township supervisor. He would remain secure in who God made him to be and act on his God-given gifts and talents to faithfully discharge the duties of the office of supervisor according to the best of his ability. He'd do his best to keep the lines of communication open and honest as he attended the township board meetings, and yes, receive the complaints, ideas, and suggestions concerning township affairs. From now on, he would operate out of knowing his security was wrapped up in his intimate relationship with God as his Father, not in what others said or thought about him. He had passed the test.

Endnotes

1.   Dr. John C. Maxwell, "Why insecure leaders are so bad," Excerpt from Dr. John C. Maxwell's free monthly e-newsletter 'Leadership Wired' available at www.MaximumImpact.com (Accessed March 2009).

2.   Ibid.

3.   Ibid.

4.   "John Maxwell's Laws of Leadership," *Harry Tucker—Observations and Musings,* http://harrytucker.blogspot.com/2008/06/john-maxwell-laws-of-leadership.html (Accessed April 7, 2009).

The Security Test

Personal reflection questions/discussion

1. Describe a time you have felt insecure as a leader. What were the precipitating events and how did they connect to your personal feelings of insecurity?

2. Can you see yourself in any of the "characteristics that insecure leaders have in common" in this chapter? Which ones? What steps of healing have you taken?

3. How do you react to those who rebel against your leadership? Does your reaction come from insecurity as a leader?

4. How has your anointing (calling) as a leader caused you to be secure?

5. Describe a time you realized that failure is only an event, not who you are.

—ɷ—

The Grace Test

Effective leaders know success depends on the grace of God.

Hayden was a highly successful corporate lawyer. He not only had a knack for understanding business people's desire of having well-drafted contracts, but he also stood out in the crowd because he had an ability to make the client feel that the fee paid to him was a worthwhile "investment." And he was awarded handsomely for his efforts. As a Christian man, he was consciousness and hard-working—the kind of person who got things done and who did not take advantage of clients.

At an early age he had become managing partner at his firm, running the firm for 20 years as it grew in size. He loved his career, which gave him the chance to use his brain for problem-solving work and to fight for his clients and help them achieve their business objectives. At age 55 he turned over the managing partner position to a colleague. Two years later, the firm collapsed. Hayden's job of 20 years was gone.

His first instinct was to think, *God, I've served you all these years, I've built up this firm, I've been faithful and a person of integrity on the job, why are you allowing the bottom to drop out? Don't I deserve better for all those years of service? Don't You owe me for my faithfulness to You?*

Then Hayden caught himself. He realized his thinking was all wrong. This was a test of grace. Did he, or did he not believe that he was successful because of what he had done—or was it simply because of God's grace on his life? What did grace mean, really?

When I was younger, I did not understand grace at all. I thought God really owed me something. "Look, God," I thought, "I've given you my life. I've given you everything. I've given you my family. It all belongs to you." I was working 60 hours on a job in addition to being involved with a youth ministry. I thought, "God, you have to take care of my family. You have to take care of my relationship with my wife. After all, I'm serving you; I'm giving you my life."

Then I received a revelation from the Lord about the grace of God; it revolutionized my life. I realized that God didn't *owe* me anything. God did not owe me a strong marriage or a healthy family or a large ministry. But even though I did not deserve it, God wanted to give me a strong marriage and family and ministry because of His awesome grace. Grace comes as a gift of God. Unlike a birthday gift that we receive in recognition of an event, grace is given to us by God for no reason. We cannot earn it; it is a gift. Grace is the unconditional love of God for us, exactly as we are, apart from our own efforts.

If we think we deserve our prosperous business, growing church, godly children, a good job, and good friends because we have done all the right things, we are sorely wrong! I am thankful that God has given me so many blessings in this life including a wonderful family and marriage and ministry, but it is not because of anything that I have done. I am simply a recipient of the grace of God that I have received from Him as a free gift.

Charles was a hard-driving Christian business owner. Along with his partners he had built a business from scratch. He believed that with hard work, integrity, and grit he could accomplish almost anything. Charles was known as the hardest working man in the company. He always delivered results. He had little patience for failure or weakness. He believed he could overcome any obstacle and was frequently annoyed when others in the company demonstrated weakness. Charles was a healthy and fit man; however, one day an unexpected physical condition totally incapacitated him and placed him flat on his back in a hospital bed. In excruciating pain Charles was totally helpless. For several weeks, even after returning to his home, he had to totally rely on his wife and others to meet even his most basic needs. Charles suddenly developed a new understanding of the fact that he could get out of bed in the morning only as a result of the grace of God. Charles now understands that anything and everything he accomplishes is a result of God's grace. He has more grace and understanding for the weaknesses and challenges of others.

From start to finish, we must live our lives in God's grace. God's grace through faith brings salvation to us at the start of our Christian lives and continues giving us the power and ability to respond to God and resist sin. Grace is a wonderful gift that God gives because He loves us!

God's grace offered in the Scriptures goes far beyond what is offered by other world religions. Many religions say that man gets what he deserves. Others add that man does not get all that he deserves (mercy). Grace goes way beyond that idea, however. Grace is God's unimaginable and total kindness. We receive it freely and do not deserve it, and our hearts cannot help but change because of it. We cannot fully describe it, but we can experience it. Grace affects everything we do in life.

A few years ago, I was traveling through a small town in the Midwest with my family. I was not aware the speed limit was 25 miles per hour, and I was traveling 35 miles per hour. As I got to the other side of the town, I heard a shrill siren behind me. Sure enough it was a policeman, signaling me to pull off to the side of the road. He then proceeded to write up a traffic ticket as he fulfilled his responsibility as a police officer. Now, if the policeman would have been exercising mercy, he would have said, "Look, I understand you didn't realize you were going 10 miles per hour over the limit. I'll allow you to go free." If he would have been operating in a principle of grace, he would have said, "You are a really nice guy. In fact, I like you so much I'd like to give you a hundred dollars just for traveling on our streets." Unfortunately for me, he did not operate in mercy or grace, but he did allow me to receive *justice*—he gave me a ticket with a fine to pay!

When I finally began to understand the grace of God, it changed the way I thought, acted, and responded to difficulties that arose in my life. In First Corinthians 15:10, Paul the apostle tells us that *"by the grace of God I am what I am..."* (NIV). Are you having problems? It would be much worse except for the grace of God. Are things going really well? If your business grows by leaps and bounds or your church grows from five to five thousand—it is all by the grace of God!

Do we feel we are successful or things go well for us because we pray a lot or because we have done our homework (been diligent) or because we picked the right people to help us or because we have a high IQ? Or are we convinced that although the Lord does use these things in our lives, we are still completely dependent upon the grace of God? This is the grace test!

And the other side of the grace test is to know that we can do anything He asks us to do because He gives us the grace to do it—even those hard things we think are impossible. We can do all things through Christ who strengthens us. Christ lives in us.

Leaders Are Totally Dependent on God's Grace

Paul the apostle went through years of theological training and had an impeccable background of pure Jewish descent. He was "someone." Yet he says that all his advantages of birth, education, and personal achievement can be attributed to the grace of God:

> *But whatever I am now, it is all because God poured out His special favor on me—and not without results. For I*

have worked harder than any of the other apostles; yet it was not I but God who was working through me by His grace (1 Corinthians 15:10).

Sometimes we think we have to come up with 15-second infomercials about ourselves that show we are out-of-the-ordinary, exemplary leaders. We will casually toss out some facts about ourselves like, "I was a missionary in the jungles of Peru for ten years, after which I pastored a megachurch in Texas for 15 years. Now I lecture at State University and tutor inner-city kids on the weekends and supervise a soup kitchen in my community." If we start to believe our own press releases and think we are rather fantastic spiritual leaders or husbands or gifted business and community leaders, we have gotten caught up in trying to show that we are worthy of God's love and grace.

We must remember our strength is not in ourselves, but in Jesus Christ. Like Paul, we are totally dependent on the grace of God. Everything that we have, everything that we will ever do, everything that we are, is simply by the grace of God. I know a young man who is at the top of his academic high school class, yet he says his intelligence comes from God. He knows it is a gift from God, and this will take him far.

Everything that we have, everything that we will ever do, everything that we are, is simply by the grace of God.

When we understand how grace works in our lives, we will find ourselves living with a new freedom in our daily relationship with Jesus. Every good thing in our lives is a result of the grace of God. You and I really do not deserve anything. If you have good health today, it is because of the grace of God. Any gift or ability you have can be credited to the grace of God. If you are an excellent parent, it is not because you are so talented with children, but it is the grace of God that enables you to be a good parent. If you are a fantastic basketball player, it's because of the grace of God. You may say, "But I practice." Who gave you the ability and health to practice?

God did. Good students are recipients of the grace of God. If you are a financially secure businessman, the grace of God is the reason that you are successful. When we get this truth into our spirits and live out the grace of God, it totally revolutionizes us. It changes us from the inside out.

The devil cannot puff you up with pride if you understand the grace of God. People who are proud are really saying, "I am the reason things are working so well," and they look to themselves instead of to God. People who are living in the grace of God are always looking to Jesus. They are living with a sense of thankfulness, knowing that He's the One who has given them every good gift and every good thing they have.

Grace Can "Do the Impossible"

The other side of God's grace is defined as the power and desire to do God's will. The grace of God is a kind of divine power that the Holy Spirit releases in our lives.

In the Scriptures, Zerubbabel was faced with a formidable challenge (see Ezra 3). When Cyrus the king allowed the Jews to return to their own land, he appointed Zerubbabel to be the governor of the colony. One of Zerubbabel's first responsibilities was to lay the foundation for the new temple. However, due to opposition from the enemies of the Jews, the work on this project soon ceased.

Doesn't that sound familiar to us as leaders? We get a vision from the Lord or begin to take a direction in life, and before long we receive opposition, become discouraged, and quit. Or maybe we don't quit, but we seem to find it impossible to complete the task that we believe the Lord has laid before us. This is where grace comes in!

One day Zechariah the prophet was given a vision from the Lord. As he describes his vision in Zechariah 4:6-7 (NKJV), an angel of the Lord gives Zechariah a prophetic message for Zerubbabel:

> *Not by might nor by power, but by my Spirit," says the Lord of Hosts. "Who are you, O great mountain? Before*

Zerubbabel you shall become a plain! And he shall bring forth the capstone with shouts of 'Grace, grace to it!'

The work on the temple was resumed and completed four years later. The Lord gave them "divine energy," and the circumstances supernaturally changed for them to complete the entire project. That which seemed impossible literally happened before their very eyes. They no longer trusted in their own ability, but in the grace of God. As they released divine energy by shouting, "Grace, grace," the *mountain* before them became a *great plain*. They were convinced that the temple was built not by military might or by political power or by human strength, but by the Spirit of the Lord. They had experienced the grace of God!

We can only do God's work if we are enabled by the Holy Spirit. I dare you to apply this scriptural principle to your life. The next time a mountain of impossibility stares you in the face, shout "Grace, grace" to it. See the mountain leveled as you take an act of simple faith and shout "Grace, grace" in the face of the devil. You will find your focus changing from your ability (or lack of ability) to His ability.

Some time ago, I ministered to a group of university student leaders. We stood together and proclaimed, "Grace, grace" over every university campus represented at the conference. Faith arose in our hearts as our dependency was no longer in our own strategies and abilities but in the living God.

I find it refreshing to walk into our offices and hear staff persons declaring, "Grace, grace" in the midst of deadlines that seem impossible to meet. My faith is increased when fathers proclaim, "Grace, grace" over their families. Striving is replaced by a sense of peace and rest in the Lord.

When the children of Israel shouted, "Grace, grace" to the temple, they did not sit around and wait for the walls to be built by an angel. They had a renewed sense that as they worked together fulfilling the plan of God, it was not by their own might or power, but by the Spirit of the Lord that the walls were being built. As we proclaim, "Grace,

grace" over our lives and ministries, we do not receive a license to be lazy. Instead, we receive divine energy to fulfill the purposes of God for our lives.

All Credit Goes to God

Leaders will never take credit for what God does in their ministries, businesses, or families if they understand His grace. For example, I have had the privilege of ministering to many people throughout the world in the past few years. It has been such a blessing to see people's lives changed by the power of God. I could never take credit for that. I know it is only by the grace of God that I can minister the good news of Jesus Christ.

The Bible tells us we are all competent ministers (see 2 Cor. 3:5); we are called to help other people and minister in Jesus' name. It's not us ministering to others in our own strength, but God who lives inside of us ministering through us. You and I are called to be channels of God's love.

Electric wire is a channel for electric power. We don't see an electric line and think, "What a beautiful wire." No, we are just thankful for the power that comes through the wire. Likewise, we are channels of the Holy Spirit, and we can never take credit for anything that God does. We must allow His grace and power to flow from our lives. We have been chosen as heirs of Christ to carry His banner, "*having been justified by His grace*" (Titus 3:7 NKJV). What an awesome privilege—of all the people in the world, He has chosen you and me!

I encourage you to begin to shout "Grace, grace" to the mountains in your life. Remember Zerubbabel? He knew that the grace of God would be released and the people would get the job completed quickly, effectively, and efficiently if he was obedient. So the people shouted, "Grace, grace" to the temple, and it was completed, causing great excitement among the people. They realized that it wasn't their strength, but the strength of God's grace working through them.

No matter what situation you find yourself in, you need to learn to speak "Grace, grace" to it. If you have a habit you want to conquer, but have repeatedly fallen flat on your face, begin to speak grace to that situation. Maybe you are a businessperson and are struggling financially. Begin to speak grace to your business. Perhaps you are encouraging a new believer who is under pressure with some area of his or her life. Begin to speak grace to that area. Is there a conflict in your marriage? Maybe you are a single person and have a special need. Begin to speak grace to your life. Maybe your prayer life needs revitalizing. Speak grace to your prayer life.

Begin to speak grace to your life.

The grace of God affects us every day. We need to be sure never to take it for granted. Only we can block the grace of God from flowing through our lives. If we find ourselves outside the grace of God, we are urged to be reconciled to God (see 2 Cor. 5:20).

Leaders who are in tune with their flaws are more patient and understanding when others fail. They know how to give themselves the grace to get back on the road again and learn from mistakes, and they extend that grace to others.

We can be victorious in every area of life—in our homes, in school, in our small groups and churches, and in our places of business. God has given us supernatural provision to live an overcomer's life by His abundance of grace. We do not deserve any of it, but the Lord pours it on us anyway.

As we come humbly before God as leaders, let's ask that by His grace we may walk as Jesus did, humbly and lovingly serving others.

—⁓—

Hayden quickly came to the conclusion that God did not owe him anything. He knew deep inside that it was all because of grace that he even became a lawyer and gained any kind of success in his field.

As it turned out, God's grace was in the whole process of change coming. Most of the lawyers in his firm turned down great offers of employment elsewhere after their firm failed. Instead, they used their own money as collateral and signed for a bank loan to get started as they chose to stay together as a team. They formed a new firm that grew and prospered. Hayden realized just how much grace affects everything in life. He needed the grace of God for his daily walk with God. Hayden would trust God to provide daily strength through His grace working in him.

The Grace Test

Personal reflection questions/discussion

1. What areas of your life do you presently need to speak "grace, grace" to?

2. How are you totally dependent on God's grace?

3. Describe a time you experienced God's divine energy of grace to do the impossible. What kind of test did you have to go through to experience it?

4. Why is it that leaders who are in tune with their flaws are more in tune to grace?

—⁂—

Chapter 15

The Expectations Test

Effective leaders avoid unmet expectations.

Dave and Josh met playing football at Golden State. They just clicked. When Josh's dad invited his son Josh to join Diamond Technology, a small start-up company, after college, he immediately thought of Dave as the right person to join him in this venture. Initially, Dave loved his new job leading the manufacturing arm of the business.

But gradually something changed dramatically. He now felt he was being held to an impossible standard. Lately he had experienced an avalanche of criticism from both the company owners and from many of the other employees he was overseeing. He realized he was not a gifted administrator. His gifts were in public relations and in helping the team leaders with people problems. But the expectations his employers and fellow employees had for him as a leader really went beyond what was ever stated in his job description, he thought.

As a matter of fact, these expectations were not in writing. His fellow employees and others in management just assumed he knew about them. Now that he failed to meet their expectations, tensions flared. The owners felt he was disorganized and lazy because he missed meetings and came unprepared. It wasn't that he didn't care, he just didn't love meetings. He would much rather be involved in "management by walking around," dealing with people issues rather than sitting in boring meetings.

He felt ready to give up. Yet he knew he couldn't. He did not want to be a quitter. But the unmet expectations that he was experiencing were just overwhelming. He didn't want to fail as a leader; he wanted to grow as a leader. What steps could he take to make this all work?

Dave was faced with expectations that others had of him that were not being met. And Dave was also not experiencing what he had expected when he took this job. Welcome to the world of unmet expectations!

—॥॥—

So many families, marriages, churches, ministries, and businesses are not fulfilling their God-given destiny because of experiencing the disappointment of unmet expectations. The issue of unmet expectations chokes the life from us—a wife that expected Prince Charming and got a man who hasn't grown up yet, the hard-working employee who was overlooked for a promotion, a leader who expects God to do something a certain way and it didn't work out that way at all.

When our expectations are not met, we can become deeply disappointed.

The key Scripture this entire biblical concept is built upon is Hebrews 12:15: *"Look after each other so that none of you fails to receive the grace of God. Watch out that no poisonous root of bitterness grows up to trouble you, corrupting many."* When our expectations are not met, we can become deeply disappointed. If those unmet expectations take root and plant a root of bitterness deep in our hearts, it will choke out our dreams and vision and the blessings that God wants to give us.

Great Expectations

As a leader, you must gain awareness of your internal desires and motivations. These are your expectations. You have expectations of yourself. You have expectations of others. And there are expectations that others have of you. If you do not clearly disclose your desires and preferences to those around you, you will resent it when they fail to meet those needs or fail to understand you. Even if you say what you expect of others, they may not understand. Often the result is miscommunication problems along with frustrating mixed signals. Both parties start to resent each other. That's where the root of bitterness starts to grow.

Do you realize that the plan of the enemy is to keep you from fulfilling your destiny? Why do great leaders sometimes fall into horrible sin and make terrible decisions? In many cases, it is directly related to unmet expectations. This whole process does not happen overnight, but through small steps, not unlike the proverbial frog in the kettle of water who doesn't know he is being boiled.

Unmet expectations often begin with disappointment and continue on with anger, hurt, helplessness, and low self-esteem.

Unmet expectations often begin with disappointment and continue on with anger, hurt, helplessness, and low self-esteem. Sometimes we have expectations of what we felt God would do for us, and it didn't happen. Or we may have expectation of ourselves that we haven't fulfilled, and we feel disappointed. We may be disappointed with our spouse, our church, our children, or another Christian leader. The list goes on and on.

If we forgive and release and apply the grace of God to our lives, we will receive grace from the Lord and find steps to freedom. We can go back to the first stage of unmet expectations that is filled with disappointment and forgive ourselves and others. We can release those unmet expectations and then walk in freedom.

But if we do not forgive, we will soon begin experiencing discontentment. The grass begins looking greener on the other side of the fence. We become negative. We stop seeing the positive in our lives and in the lives of others. When we enter into negativity, we are no longer sure we can trust people again, because of someone who has hurt us. Or we may find it much harder to trust God than in the past. Perhaps a prayer was not answered in the way we had thought it should be answered.

> **One of the main hindrances to effective leadership happens when our wants and needs—our expectations—are threatened.**

Proverbs 13:12 describes the pain of unfulfilled expectations, *"Hope deferred makes the heart sick...."* Like the writer of this proverb, many leaders experience the pain of longing for something that forever seems out of reach. We know the pain of hard work toward a goal that is never actualized. We thought we expressed our needs and expectations, but they were ignored, dismissed, or outright defied. It is in those times that the heart feels sick. The difference between our assumptions and theirs leaves us with unmet expectations, and it starts to affect the way we relate to others. One of the main hindrances to effective leadership happens when our wants and needs—our expectations—are threatened.

The Rough Road of Unmet Expectations

Every leader goes through the rough road of unmet expectations. Sometimes it seems as if they may not get repaired anytime soon, as this author realized:

> The road by my house was in bad condition after a rough winter. Every day I dodged potholes on the way to work.

So I was relieved to see a construction crew working on the road one morning. Later, on my way home, I noticed no improvement. But where the construction crew had been working stood a new, bright-yellow sign with the words 'Rough Road.'[1]

As we travel through life, it may seem as if there is just a "rough road" sign posted and the repairs have not been made. Life is filled with rough spots, and we will continue to face disappointments, but we don't have to be devastated when our expectations aren't met. What we need to learn is that having expectations is normal and not the problem. How we deal with unmet expectations is what can make or break our relationships.

If we instead take our hearts, broken in disappointment, to God, He will restore us and give us the ability to love unconditionally the ones we perceived have failed us. When we realize we must live for God alone, seeking only His approval, it will be amazing to see how our relationships will succeed in a way that they did not while we had expectations of them.

I am a promoter. I love to help others fulfill their dreams, but sometimes I have given others unmet expectations by telling them the potential I see in them without laying out the requirements they will need to see that vision fulfilled. As leaders, we must be careful of what we speak. If we speak vision over people's lives concerning what we see in them, and it does not come to pass in the time frame they expected, or they do not know how to go about fulfilling the dream, they will be hurt and disappointed. We need to be careful that we do not set in motion expectations that cannot be met, which can lead to disappointment.

In the Church and in business, we often hope the people we serve with will continue to serve with us for a long time. When people leave, it can be a test for us. Once while I was in Hawaii I sat with a pastor and his wife; she blurted out, "I hate last suppers!"

"What is a last supper?" I asked.

"When people in the church take us out for a meal and then tell us why they are leaving our church!" she said. This pastor, like most, had the expectation that his members would be loyal and stay and support the church, but it does not always work out that way. People will leave. If the pastor's faith remains in Christ, he can face those disappointments and won't be devastated when his expectations are not met. We must guard our hearts from taking an offense when personal expectations are not met. We must forgive others because the Lord has forgiven us. Forgiveness and speaking blessing to those who have hurt or disappointed us will cause us to pass this test. And remember, forgiving does not mean that what they did was right. It was probably wrong. But forgiveness releases both us and the one who has hurt us to experience the Lord's intervention in our lives.

We must respond to the unmet expectations of life in ways that create solutions by finding ways to heal the wounds of letdowns and injustices. Ask the Lord to give you the desire and willingness to release your expectations of yourself and others, to not insist on your own way, and to compromise and to adjust. Ask the Lord to soften your heart!

―⚏―

The unmet expectations between Dave and Josh and the other company owners and employees had led to a growing sense of failure, frustration, and even depression on Dave's part. He was concerned he might get fired. He was determined not to allow the gap between his own expectations and the expectations of others at Diamond Technologies to become too great. They were already experiencing increasing tension. Since administration was not his strength, Dave realized that he must be honest and open with both the owners and his fellow employees about what he was experiencing. He forgave his fellow employees in his heart, received grace from God, and his attitude began to change. He knew that he had to find out what was really expected of him and build a team that would allow others' strengths to shine where he was weak. He made a commitment that he would work through his feelings of failure and the awkward staff meetings. He appealed to the owners, and they began for the first time to write job descriptions for employees. He found a trusted mentor who had experienced much of what he was presently experiencing ten years prior, and this friend gave him clear steps to take. He would not bail out and give up. Instead, he would do what leaders do in time of crisis—he would lead his department through the rough road.

Endnote

1.   Sarah Kraybill Lind, "Rough Driving," *Reader's Digest,* http://www.rd.com/clean-jokes-and-laughs/rough-driving-joke/article86208.html (Accessed April 7, 2009).

The Expectations Test

Personal reflection questions/discussion

1. Describe how unmet expectations can either become demands or disappointments.

2. Are you aware of your internal desires and expectations as a leader? Do you clearly make these known to others?

3. Describe a time others had expectations of you as a leader, and you failed them.

4. Describe a time you had expectations of someone, and they failed to meet those expectations.

5. How have you endeavored to find solutions so that your unmet expectations can be healed?

—ɯ—

Chapter 16

The Finance Test

*Effective leaders take fiscal responsibility for
their mission.*

Vince and Darlene knew they were called to the mission field of
Indonesia. They had been planning, dreaming, and training since
they graduated from college three years ago. Now all they needed to do
was to raise their monthly support and they could get on with their missionary calling! They knew that raising the funds to go would be a challenge, but they had a wide circle of friends, family, and church family
whom they were sure would embrace them. They had no doubts that
God had called them, and He would provide. The plan was to receive
donor support channeled through their church.

They excitedly sent out their support letters, made countless phone
calls, and spoke at local churches. They operated out of the motivation that
they and their supporters would be on a journey together, each having a
part in the work. They tried to make everyone feel like they would be an
important part.

The fund-raising went well at first. Friends and family were enthusiastic. But they now had reached a standstill in raising support. What was pledged each month was only partial support for the two of them. It would not be enough.

Vince and Darlene's energy and enthusiasm for support-raising floundered. They felt deeply disappointed that God had not met their monthly quota. Hadn't they taken a 70 percent pay cut from their earning potential already by choosing to serve on the mission field? Was their missionary dream going to fizzle out because of a lack of finances? Did they have enough of faith to believe for more? It was a financial test they were not sure they would pass!

Have you noticed that many times when the topic of money or finances comes up in Church settings, there seems to be an uneasy feeling that spreads across the group? Why do we feel this way? What is this uncomfortable feeling? Could this feeling be a spirit of poverty that aims to strip the Church of one of the tools it needs and God wants to supply—money?

In his book *Prosperity with a Purpose,* my colleague and friend, Brian Sauder, says that we have more available to us in the area of financial provision than we often ask for.

> Listen to Paul's words as he is writing to the Ephesian Christians.
>
> *I pray also that the eyes of your heart may be enlightened in order that you may know the hope to which he has called you, the riches of his glorious inheritance in the saints, and his incomparably great power for us who believe* [Ephesians 1:18-19 NIV].

Somehow the Ephesian Christians were missing part of their inheritance. Paul was praying for their eyes to be opened to it.

Is it possible that we, like the Ephesians, have missed part of our inheritance in Christ? Has the progress of our mission been slowed because we haven't asked for the tools we need to complete it? Has the spirit of poverty blinded our eyes and kept us from even asking for the finances needed to do the job?[1]

> **Money is simply a tool God gives us to complete the job He has assigned us to do.**

Money is simply a tool God gives us to complete the job He has assigned us to do. Our job is called the *Great Commission*. If we closely examine the Bible, we find it talks about natural riches as well as spiritual riches. What good are all the spiritual riches in the world if we don't have the natural riches to get them to the people who need them?

Breaking Out of Survival Mode

The Church has to change its way of thinking in the area of finances, and the leaders need to lead the way. How will our thinking change? By comparing our thoughts to the Word of God. We need to renew our minds to embrace what the Scriptures say about finances. Money is a good thing that God wants to give us to help accomplish His mission for us.

The Bible tells us in First Timothy 6:10: *"For the love of money is the root of all kinds of evil. And some people, craving money, have wandered from the true faith and pierced themselves with many sorrows."* Both having too *much money* or too *little money* can be a test for us. I have met people who have passed and failed each of these tests.

Money is a very spiritual thing. We need money to purchase food and clothing and necessities for our families. One of every seven verses in the New Testament has to do with the right and wrong use of money and handling financial possessions.[2] There is a fine line between biblical prosperity and materialism.

We must be people of faith who think outside of the box. Many church leaders think only in terms of receiving tithes and offerings to meet the needs in the church, but maybe they should think in terms of multiple streams of income to meet their needs personally and for the church. For example, my friend Scott Walsh, who is a pastor in New Jersey, bought an entire building complex and is renting out much of it, allowing the rest of the property to be used for the church he pastors.

Trusting God

I believe God will test us in our faith to believe Him for the finances needed to provide for our families, to help those less fortunate than we are, to expand the Kingdom of God, and to experience the dreams the Lord has placed on our hearts. Two major financial tests are learning to trust God for "His plan" and trusting God for "His intervention."

God will test us in our faith to believe Him for the finances needed.

Moses and the Israelites trusted God in faith for daily provision. They trusted Him for the intervention He exhibited each day by providing manna in the wilderness, water from the rock, and so forth. On the other hand, Joshua and the Israelites trusted God to meet them by sowing crops and receiving the harvest—this was God's plan to provide for them. Both ways are from God, but it is up to God as to how He provides, not us. A business person lives "by faith" when he takes out a loan for a new business as much as a missionary lives "by faith" when he raises money for support. We should not consider one area of provision as more spiritual than another. If we trust any one area as being more spiritual, we are taking our eyes off of the Lord. The important aspect is that we *trust!*

Jenn learned that God is far more capable of providing for her needs than she could ever imagine. She had arthroscopic surgery on her left knee due to a skiing accident. Numerous people, including the doctor's assistant, believed that because it was a preexisting injury it would probably not be covered by her insurance policy. So Jenn and her husband began to pray. When they received the papers from the insurance company, what they had feared came true. Jenn recalls,

> I looked through the piles of bills that I thought I was going to have to pay. It came to approximately twelve thousand dollars! I panicked. I thought God had not answered our prayers. For a few days after that, I was depressed and wondered how we were going to pay for it. We got together with my parents later that week, and they looked over the papers. They soon discovered that I had been mistaken. Those bills were just copies of what the insurance company had paid. The surgery had been covered![3]

How God Fills Our Cups

How does the Lord desire to fill your cup to provide for you and for your family? Luke 6:38 tells us:

> *Give, and you will receive. Your gift will return to you in full—pressed down, shaken together to make room for more, running over, and poured into your lap* [filling your cup]. *The amount you give will determine the amount you get back.*

We must allow the Lord to fill our cup any way He chooses. Luke 16:10-11 teaches us that God uses our proper handling of money to prepare us for spiritual ministry.

I believe that God's plan to finance the local church is through the tithes (10 percent) and offerings (see Mal. 3:8-11; Matt. 23:23). However, when a new church is being planted, there usually are not enough tithes to support a leader for the church. If you are a leader of a new church or are starting a ministry, your cup may be filled by a combination of sources. Here are some of the ways (potential sources of provision) the Lord may choose to fill your financial cup:

Tent-Making

"He stayed with them and worked…" (Acts 18:1-3 NKJV). Tent-making is working at a job or business to earn income to finance our family and the new church plant as the church is being planted.

Supernatural Provision

In Matthew 17:27, Peter found a coin in the mouth of a fish to pay his taxes and Jesus' taxes. This was not normal for Jesus' provision; however, the Lord did feed the 5,000 supernaturally.

Support Team of Family and Friends

In Luke 8:1-3, we read that Jesus had a team who supported Him from their substance. Many ministries encourage missionaries and church planters to build a support team, send out newsletters, etc. This is a scriptural way for the Lord to provide.

Local Church Support

In Second Corinthians 8:3-4, a gift was given to Paul from the local church. Some missionaries and church planters are blessed by the support of their local church as God's way of providing for them.

Living From the Gospel

First Corinthians 9:7-14 teaches us that those who preach the Gospel should live from the Gospel. Galatians 6:6 says, *"Let him who is taught the word share in all good things with him who teaches"* (NKJV). If a traveling minister (see Eph. 4:11-12) preaches the Word of God to a home group or local church, the believers should bless him financially. This helps to fill his cup.

"Honor" Given to a Leader Who Is Sent Out

First Timothy 5:17-18 tells us the laborer is worthy of his wages. Sometimes a local church leader will be supported by his home church as he ministers for a season in another part of the world.

Inheritance

Proverbs 13:22 says a good man leaves an inheritance to his children's children. Some families have used inheritance money as God's provision to support them as short-term missionaries and church planters.

Investments and Business

In Matthew 25:14-18, Jesus gives the Parable of the Talents. Some successful businessmen who have been blessed to use their talents wisely give a season of their lives to missions and church planting. Retired military personnel have at times used their pension to support them financially in church planting and missions.

The Ant Method (Work and Save)

Proverbs 6:6-8 tells us that ants *"labor hard in the summer, gathering food for the winter"* (TLB). Some missionaries and church planters work hard and save for a season and then use the money that is saved to support themselves on the mission field and in church planting.

Kingdom Breadwinning

Luke 10:7 tells us the laborer is worthy of his wages. "Kingdom breadwinning" is when a person is paid by the church or Christian ministry where he serves as a staff member of that church or ministry.[4]

Taking Personal Responsibility for Finances

In the news today, there has been an abundance of bad news reported about business leaders taking astronomical bonuses for poor performance. We hear about major corporate leaders asking for government bailout money with their left hand while continuing to spend money frivolously with the right hand. It seems no one wants to take personal responsibility for their actions.

Church leaders and ministry leaders especially know that it is their responsibility to be good stewards of whatever compensation they receive. An undisciplined financial life undermines a pastor's effectiveness in ministry. Proverbs 21:5 from the Bible offers very good advice. It says, *"The plans of the diligent lead to profit...."* (NIV).

Leaders must plan and take responsibility for their finances and those of their church or ministry and not take an entitlement mentality. Although it is normal to expect to be rewarded for your labor, if you think just because 365 days have passed you should have an increase in salary, you have an entitlement frame of mind. If you think you deserve more and more because you are working so hard and you deserve it, you have an entitlement mentality. Jesus asked His disciples to surrender all their aspirations of privilege or entitlement as leaders. He said as servants in the Kingdom they should not expect to be served, thanked, or praised (see Luke 17:7-10).

It All Belongs to Him

Many pastors today are going into business part-time and developing multiple streams of income. The false wall between the sacred and the secular is being shattered. At the same time, many business people and business owners are seeing their business as a primary place of ministry, ministering to employees and clients who would never think of going to a local church building every Sunday. These business persons are beginning to pastor their employees and their clients.

My friends, Christian business owners Lamar and his wife Nancy are the kind of employers who see their place of business as a place of ministry. They not only offer personal counseling to their employees, they also hired an intercessor to come and pray a couple of days a week at their business so that every employee is covered in prayer. They have received a mentality of the Kingdom of God as they seek first His Kingdom in their business ventures. They realize they are merely managing God's resources as good stewards.

The young missionary couple, Vince and Darlene, were at a crossroads. They had not raised enough of money to go on the mission field. They could not go to the other side of the globe with only partial support. They desperately prayed for God's wisdom. He gave it to them! An opportunity came for them to start a handicraft company in the city in which they would minister. They went to Indonesia with partial support, and in the first year of missionary service they were instrumental in building sound financial principles in getting the fledgling company on its feet. The company made a profit—enough to fill in the gaps to pay for Vince and Darlene's support. In subsequent years, the growing company continued to support them and other missionaries as well. In addition, it provided jobs for many local women. Vince and Darlene were forever grateful that they had learned to trust God for His creative ideas of provision rather than depend on a traditional fund-raising mindset. They had passed the test.

Endnotes

1.   Brian Sauder, *Prosperity with a Purpose*, (Lititz, PA: House to House Publications, 2003), 12.

2.   "Why the Bible Talks So Much About Money," *Free Money Finance: Grow Your Net Worth*, http://www.freemoneyfinance.com/ 2009/02/why -the-bible-talks-so-much-about-money.html (accessed April 21, 2009).

3.   Jennifer Paules-Kanode, "God's Amazing Provision," *God Stories from Lancaster County* (Lancaster, PA: The Regional Church of Lancaster County, 2006), 33.

4.   Brian Sauder & Larry Kreider, *Helping You Build* (Lititz, PA: House to House Publications, 2004).

The Finance Test

Personal reflection questions/discussion

1. How can we think outside the box when it comes to trusting God for finances?

2. Explain the difference between trusting God for "His intervention" and trusting Him for "His plan."

3. How has God "filled your cup" to provide for you as a leader?

4. Why is it important to take responsibility for your finances and not have an entitlement mentality?

5. How can you develop multiple streams of income as a leader?

—⌇—

Chapter 17

The Comparison Test

Effective leaders only compare up.

The business seminar was dragging on, and Lucas's thoughts started to wander. He glanced over at the other attendees and noticed an old college buddy, Alexander. Alexander was the CEO of a Fortune 500 company. Automatically Lucas thought, "Boy, I could never have done that; I'm not that smart." Suddenly and overwhelmingly Lucas started highlighting in his mind all of his shortcomings. He immediately felt a deep sense of inadequacy. Even though Lucas had started his own small but successful company, he rarely felt adequate as its founder.

He often worried what others thought of his achievements and feared that they would find them paltry or unimportant. He was insecure about his success and feared public failure and embarrassment.

He constantly compared his company with others that seemed more successful and faster-growing. As a Christian, he was aware that he should not compare, like Paul said not to compare ourselves among ourselves, but instead to evaluate himself according to God's love and acceptance. He knew it was his low self-esteem that was keeping him from believing that God loved and cared for him and wanted the best for him. What he was doing was becoming critical of God's design for his life. He knew all these things in his mind, but his heart held him captive to his insecurities and his tendency to compare himself with others to see if he measured up. What could he do so he would not be overtaken by his negative, self-limiting, and self-defeating internal thoughts? He knew that as a leader he had to pass this test, or he would derail or seriously damage his company and those who worked for him.

—⁂—

Like Lucas, sometimes business owners or ministers go to a training day or to a conference, talk to others in their field, and end up feeling terrible. Why? They begin to compare themselves to others and start feeling defeated and depressed. The truth is—there will always be someone better than you. You may be a very successful real estate agent, but if you compare yourself with someone even more successful, you start to feel inferior. This is without reason because you are still an incredible real estate agent.

On the other hand, you can always find someone worse off than you, and this can make you feel better. But it can also lead to pride. You may be the pastor of the fastest growing church in your hometown. Other churches are not growing. This may tend to make you feel superior to the other churches in town. If you feel you are doing better than others, you fall into pride. If you feel like you are doing worse than those around you, you can suffer from feelings of inferiority. Neither pride nor inferiority are grace-filled responses. The problem with comparing is that it always ends up creating something negative. It either makes you think you are better than others or more often makes you feel envious or jealous of others.

A pastor from years gone by relates this story of what happened when he decided to pray for rather than compare his church with other more successful ones in his city:

F. B. Meyer was pastor of Christ's Church in London at the time that G. Campbell Morgan was pastor of Westminster Chapel and Charles H. Spurgeon was pastor of the Metropolitan Chapel. Both Morgan and Spurgeon often had much larger audiences than did Meyer. Troubled by envy, Meyer confessed that not until he began praying for his colleagues did he have peace of heart. "When I prayed for their success," said Meyer, "the result was that God filled their churches so full that the overflow filled mine, and it has been full since."[1]

When this pastor started to pray for the prosperous churches, rather than allow envy to fill his heart, his church also became successful.

Comparing Is Not Wise

Paul says that he did not dare to compare himself with other leaders like some were doing. He says that when we compare ourselves to others, we are not wise:

> We wouldn't dare say that we are as wonderful as these other men who tell you how important they are! But they are only comparing themselves with each other, using themselves as the standard of measurement. How ignorant! (2 Corinthians 10:12).

Rather than comparing ourselves with others, we should compare ourselves with the Word of God and allow the Word to dwell in us so we can live out the principles of grace in our lives.

When God uses someone else for a certain ministry or responsibility and you are not called into action, how do you respond? If you start the comparison game, you are falling short of the grace of God. God is God. He knows best what you need.

He may give somebody one gift and another person a different gift. If you question why God gives some people greater talents and abilities than others, you have not understood the grace of God. If you feel cheated that other people are packaged with more abilities than you, you do not understand God's grace. Do you ever find yourself saying things like, "I wish I could sing like Julie, I wish I could speak like Josh, I wish I could lead worship like Dan, I wish I could start a business like Loren?" If so, you are falling short of God's grace.

Do you know that geneticists tell us that no one has ever had a duplicate of your genes? Sociologists tell us no one has a duplicate of your experience. In Romans 12:6, Paul says all of us have *"different gifts."* This should keep us from comparing at all! How can we compare if we are unique and one of a kind? How can we compare the incomparable? God made you unique. He doesn't match you up to an unfair standard. He doesn't look at you and say, "Why aren't you more like Brenda?" You don't win by competing with others.

Every family and every team and every business and every church needs a diversity of people with many different gifts and abilities. Be who you were created to be! We all face the comparison test sometime in our lives, so let's be sure to compare ourselves to the Lord's plan for our lives so that we move into the *"measure of the stature of the fullness of Christ"* (Eph. 4:13 NKJV). This comparison leads to Jesus.

In Comparing, We Lose Sight of Who We Are

Remember when God told Moses to send men to explore the land of Canaan? The men came back boasting of the land's bounty, but they were fearful of its inhabitants.

> *The land we traveled through and explored will devour anyone who goes to live there. All the people we saw were huge. We even saw giants there....Next to them*

we felt like grasshoppers, and that's what they thought, too (Numbers 13:32-33).

By comparing themselves to the inhabitants, the Israelites lost sight of who they were. They lost sight of God's promise to give them the land. Their fear led to faithlessness, which caused God to become angry with them. By comparing ourselves to others we can lose sight of who we are. We can lose sight of the promises and plans God gives us. Fear of not measuring up can lead to faithlessness. That's why comparing is so destructive.

In his book *Counseling Basics,* Steve Prokopchak says that

> When we compare ourselves with others, we actually inhibit ourselves from becoming who God wants us to be. He gives gifts to us (Romans 11:29) and each of us has something to contribute. I do not gauge myself and my actions by other people's gifts and callings, but by the gifts and callings God has given me.[2]

When we compare ourselves with others, we actually inhibit ourselves from becoming who God wants us to be.

Comparing Sows Seeds of Unhealthy Competition

Keeping mental notes of the successes and failures of others sows seeds of unhealthy competition. Selfish striving, jealousy, and mistrust are born in that seedbed of wrongly focused thoughts and emotions.

According to Second Corinthians 10:5, we need to *"take captive every thought"* (NIV) by bringing all our thoughts into alignment with God's will. In "Special Ops" training in the military, trainees perform special water operations to train the mind and body to respond in that element. To train in the water, their hands are tied behind their backs and they jump into water that is over their heads. Two things are learned in this training exercise. First it cures the fear of water because you learn how to control your breathing by coming up for air at the right times. Second it teaches you how to control your mind. If your mind tells you that you need air, you will need air. If you can control your mind by focusing on the task in front of you, you can go much longer without air.

Maybe all leaders should go through a kind of "Special Ops" training that trains us to allow the Holy Spirit to manage our minds and emotions. Romans chapter 8 teaches this principle clearly by insisting that the Holy Spirit within us must be in command of our mind and emotions. Change occurs as the Spirit overrules our flesh. When we allow the Holy Spirit to direct us, we will not be tempted to compare ourselves with each other.

Rejoice for Others' Successes!

The Bible tells us to *"rejoice with those who rejoice; mourn with those who mourn"* (Rom. 12:15 NIV). Both rejoicing and mourning demand selflessness. But rejoicing with others involves a different and more difficult selflessness than mourning with them. To rejoice means that we suppress feelings of jealousy and envy. It means we are happy for others' successes.

Our whole lives are in God's hands. If we know that all things are in Jesus' hands, we can trust Him to work things out for us rather than to react negatively to the success of others. Jealousy of others can poison our own happiness. One sign of jealousy is when it's easier to show sympathy and "weep with those who weep" than it is to exhibit joy and "rejoice with those who rejoice."

Be Yourself

Every leader is on his or her own track in life, and they are all different. Our priorities are different, and God deals with us in different ways. He takes us through different routes on life's journey. In his book *Bread for the Journey,* Henri Nouwen says that we must learn to be happy with how the Lord made us and stop trying to be someone we are not.

Often we want to be somewhere other than where we are, or even to be someone other than who we are. We tend to compare ourselves constantly with others and wonder why we are not as rich, as intelligent, as simple, as generous, or as saintly as they are. Such comparisons make us feel guilty, ashamed or jealous. It is very important to realize that our vocation is hidden in where we are and who we are. We are unique human beings, each with a call to realize in life what nobody else can, and to realize it in the concrete context of the here and now. We will never find our vocations by trying to figure out whether we are better or worse than others. We are good enough to do what we are called to do. Be yourself![3]

There is really no one who is worthy of comparing yourself to but Jesus Christ.

There is really no one who is worthy of comparing yourself to but Jesus Christ. He is your only standard. He alone knows who you are and what you were made for. First John 2:6 says, *"Those who say they live in God should live their lives as Jesus did."* Forget about trying to fit into someone else's mold. God made us all different. You can be comfortable with how God made you as a leader.

—⁓—

Lucas was tired of feeling incompetent to handle life's challenges and the fear that his weaknesses would be discovered. His insecurities and tendency to compare were sabotaging his leadership at his company. Through the help of trusted friends and counselors, he realized that comparing himself and his business success to others is rooted in pride. It took diligent prayer and heart-searching, but Lucas came to realize that because he had submitted himself to God, he was now spiritually transformed and conformed to the image of Christ. He must stop giving so much importance to his shortcomings. He prayed along with David the Psalmist, *"Search me, O God, and know my heart: try me, and know my anxieties; and see if there is any wicked way in me, and lead me in the way everlasting"* (Ps. 139:23-24 NKJV). His attitudes started to change slowly, before his self-evaluation was flawed. But now he was comparing himself to a pure and righteous standard—God's. He had passed the test of comparison.

Endnotes

1. "Eliminating Envy," A Meditation on Proverbs 3:31, 14:30, 23:17, http://www.foxlakechurch.org/fox%20lake%20community%20church_016.htm, accessed July 29, 2009.

2. Steve Prokopchak, *Counseling Basics* (Lititz, PA: House to House Publications, 2004), 26.

3. Henri J. M. Nouwen, *Bread for the Journey* (New York: HarperCollins, 1997), 18.

The Comparison Test

Personal reflection questions/discussion

1. Think of a time you compared yourself to another leader. Were these feelings of inadequacy or pride?

2. Have you ever questioned God about why He gave someone else a better gift than yours? Was this kind of comparison ever fruitful?

3. How does comparing ourselves with others cause us to lose sight of who we are?

4. Describe how you passed a test of comparison.

5. How does comparing sow seeds of unhealthy competition?

6. How easy is it for you to rejoice for others' successes? This is a test!

—⚡—

Chapter 18

The Perseverance Test

Effective leaders refuse to quit!

Kara was a community organizer for breast cancer awareness in her district. She was a director that liked to take express action and get things done. She had a knack for recruiting people and funds. She was a dedicated, visionary person who was willing to work hard for something she believed in—to raise money to fund a cure for breast cancer. Although not a breast cancer survivor herself, she knew what it was like to persevere in the face of odds. She had had her own battles. Even as a teenager, she had suffered from rheumatoid arthritis. She often experienced fatigue, low-grade fevers, and muscle and joint aches.

That's why she had never actually participated in the "Race for the Cure" event that she spent so much time raising money for. But this year, God spoke to her, "I want you to run in the 5K race this year." The thought of it was almost preposterous to Kara. She was 60 pounds overweight. "My gifts are in the office, not on the race trail," she immediately thought.

Yet Kara knew that God was trying to teach her something. She had learned many lessons about perseverance in business endeavors. But she had neglected her physical body. She had not persevered in healthy eating habits and exercise. She was weak and out of shape. Then she read one morning in Ecclesiastes 9:11: *"…The race is not to the swift, nor the battle to the strong…"* (NKJV). From that she gained courage.

She pondered, *If not all races are won by strength or swiftness, will God then give me (a weak person) the strength so that I, too, can take the prize?* Would she be able to persevere and pass the test? She breathed a prayer, *"Lord, help me not to be hindered by obstacles or limits I impose in my life. I know that You alone will give me the strength for the victory in any area of my life."*

—⚒—

You are running a race! God has given it to you to run, and it requires perseverance. It's not just a 5K race either! The race God has for you to run is more like a marathon. Paul the apostle used the analogy of a runner in a race many times in his writings. In First Corinthians 9:24-27, he says,

> *Don't you realize that in a race everyone runs, but only one person gets the prize? So run to win! All athletes are disciplined in their training. They do it to win a prize that will fade away, but we do it for an eternal prize. So I run with purpose in every step. I am not just shadowboxing. I discipline my body like an athlete, training it to do what it should. Otherwise, I fear that after preaching to others I myself might be disqualified.*

In Paul's day, athletic games were very popular. One of the major events was the Marathon, the long distance race. If you have ever run in a marathon race, you know very well that it is not a frolic in the park. It is a fight. The body wants to stop, but you urge it on. Your lungs scream for oxygen, your legs feel like noodles. In fact, the word used for *race* in the first verse above is the Greek word *agon*.[1] We get the English word *agony* from it. Running a marathon race can be pure agony. It requires perseverance that will take every ounce of energy you have and then some! Every successful leader has to pass this perseverance test.

With Perseverance, You Must Run to Win

In a race everyone runs, but only one person gets the prize. So you must run in such a way as to win! Go for the gold! Don't settle for mediocrity as a leader. You are called to run with discipline and faithfulness. Run with determination and resolution. We have all seen those leaders in the Church, in business, and in our communities who have started out strong, but soon fade away.

A runner's destination is the finish line. Your destination is the Kingdom of God, and the reward is eternal life for those who endure to the end. *"So let's not get tired of doing what is good. At just the right time we will reap a harvest of blessing if we don't give up"* (Gal. 6:9). You must run your race with perseverance and never give up, just like Beth Anne DeCiantis in her attempt to qualify for the 1992 Olympic Trials marathon (a female runner must complete the 26-mile race in less than two hours, 45 minutes).

> Beth started strong but began having trouble around mile 23. She reached the final straightaway at 2:43, with just two minutes left to qualify. Two hundred yards from the finish, she stumbled and fell. Dazed, she stayed down for twenty seconds. The crowd yelled, "Get up!" The clock was ticking—2:44, less than a minute to go.
>
> Beth Anne staggered to her feet and began walking. Five yards short of the finish, with 10 seconds to go, she fell again. She began to crawl, the crowd cheering her on,

and crossed the finish line on her hands and knees. Her time? Two hours, 44 minutes, 57 seconds.[2]

We have to seek the Lord and not get lost in mindless routine.

How do we run to win? We don't just talk about our ministry or business, we have to get our hands dirty and do it. We have to seek the Lord and not get lost in mindless routine. We make every effort to look for divine opportunities to minister to others. In this spiritual race, we win by helping others to win the race. We pray and intercede for others. We use our spiritual gifts. We press on!

Don't Get Off Track

Sometimes there are things in the race that drag us down. In an actual marathon, runners are careful not to wear clothing that weighs them down. Most runners wear performance clothing that is lightweight and wicks the moisture away from the body. Hebrews 12:1 says, *"...let us strip off every weight that slows us down, especially the sin that so easily trips us up. And let us run with endurance the race God has set before us."*

How can we strip off the weights that slow us down? The next verse tells us, *"We do this by keeping our eyes on Jesus, the champion who initiates and perfects our faith..."* (Heb. 12:2).

What happens when we take our eyes off of Jesus? We get off track. Wrong choices are made. Roy Riegals was an All-American center for the University of California football team. He has gone down in history for making a humiliating mistake in the grand final game of the 1929 season.

> Roy played both offense and defense. Close to the end of the first half, a player fumbled the ball. Roy saw his chance, scooped up the loose ball and bolted towards the goal 65 yards away.

There was one problem however. Roy was running toward the wrong goal! Fortunately, one of his teammates went after him in hot pursuit and managed to tackle him just before he crossed the opposition's goal line!

It's hard to even imagine the embarrassment and shame that Roy must have felt there on the field with thousands of startled eyes focused on him, then walking off the field with head hanging low, and sitting in the locker room with his teammates and coach during the halftime break.

In the locker room the dead silence was broken only by the sobs of the All-American star. Then Coach Price announced, "Men, the same team that started the first half will start the second half."

Roy, with red face and swollen eyes blurted out, "Coach, I can't do it. I've ruined you. I've ruined the University of California. I've ruined myself. I couldn't face that crowd in the stadium to save my life."

"Get up, Roy," the coach said. "Go back on. The game is only half over." Riegals was given a second chance, accepted it, returned to the game and gave one of the most inspiring individual efforts in Rose Bowl history![3]

Can you relate to Riegals's "going the wrong way" mistake? From Moses to Deborah to Paul to Esther to Joshua—these leaders made mistakes and had to fight their battles to make it through to the end. They were tested, but they continued on in perseverance to the end. *"I have fought the good fight, I have finished the race, I have kept the faith"* (2 Tim. 4:7 NIV). Notice the progression in this verse. When God calls us to start, He will see us through to the finish, but there is always a fight until the end!

God will provide leaders the grace to fight until the end, but not everyone receives this grace and actually finishes the race. Absolom, the handsome and promising son of King David, was called of God. But he used unholy tactics to try to steal the throne from his father and died an untimely death without accomplishing what he could have in life.

Judas, one of the 12 disciples, because of greed and demonic influences on his life, was another leader who did not finish the race or keep the faith. Today we have witnessed many national and international Christian leaders not finishing the race well because of falling into sin.

Refuse to Quit!

We all go through seasons in life. Both Church leaders and business leaders will be sure to go through at least three seasons of life—the honeymoon season, the problem season, and the perseverance-to-victory season.

The honeymoon season is the send-off, the initial start when all is new and exciting. Then the reality of the struggles involved in ministry or business hits. You could call this the problem stage because this period can bring confusion and conflict. The future is uncertain, and a leader may feel like he has entered a danger zone. Problems he never thought possible arise and sap his energy. It is during this season that he has to make a decision to deal with these problems effectively by confronting one problem at a time. It helps to separate them so they are manageable. Often during this season a leader feels like quitting. He can quit and abort the plan of God, or he can continue on in perseverance. Proverbs 24:10 says, *"If you fail under pressure, your strength is too small."*

A key posture to maintain in the perseverance stage is to "not look back." When you are driving, you keep your eyes on the road ahead—that is if you want to reach your destination intact. If you focus on what is happening behind you, you could very well end up wrapped around a telephone pole or plowed into the traffic in front of you. Focusing on our past failures and problems is mostly counterproductive. It will prevent us from moving forward. We can all look back at our lives and make the comment, "If only I had done this or that in a particular situation, maybe things would be different now." If we can see that the Lord wants to use our mistakes, trials, and tribulations for His glory, we will be able to move on; otherwise, we get discouraged and give up. Like Riegals, we must determine to regain what we have lost and stay in the game. We cannot give up.

Refuse to quit! Not quitting can be your greatest act of spiritual warfare! Charles Spurgeon once said: "With great perseverance the snail finally reached the ark."[4] Down through history, there are those who seemed like world class failures to their peers, but they persevered, and this is their legacy:

> George Washington was a general who lost two-thirds of all the battles he fought in the American Revolution.

> Abraham Lincoln lost almost every election he ran for until finally he was elected President.

> Edison tried over 200 different elements before he figured out what was the right element to use in the light bulb.

> In 21 years, Babe Ruth hit 714 home runs but he struck out 1330 times. He struck out nearly twice as often as he hit a home run. He once said, "Never let the fear of striking out keep you from taking a swing."

> A famous novelist in England, John Creasy, got 753 rejection slips from publishers before he published his first book. He went on to publish 564 books. Can you imagine the persistence?

> R.P. Macy failed seven times as an entrepreneur in retailing and then he started Macy's department store.[5]

Discipline Needed

Discipline is what keeps us going forward when our emotions are saying something different. Discipline is what causes us to "order our

187

steps" and face our fears. Paul saw himself as a runner in a race and pressed on toward the goal of knowing Christ. He knew that he could be distracted by this world's temptations and worries, but he determined to press on. *"Not that I have already obtained all this, or have already been made perfect, but I press on to take hold of that for which Christ Jesus took hold of me"* (Phil. 3:12 NIV). Such determination is necessary to go where God has called us and to press into Him.

Discipline is what keeps us going forward when our emotions are saying something different.

As a leader, press on to receive and achieve, to fulfill what Jesus Christ has destined for you. It will not just happen. There must be a pressing into Christ and a pressing on in the Spirit to fulfill all that Christ has for you. It takes discipline. Discipline is what gets us up in the morning when our bodies say, "I need sleep." Discipline keeps us fasting when our stomachs cry for food. Discipline keeps our thoughts and emotions on track when circumstances around us would dictate otherwise. Remember what Paul said in First Corinthians 9:27? *"I discipline my body like an athlete, training it to do what it should. Otherwise, I fear that after preaching to others I myself might be disqualified."*

Sometimes during our struggles in life, we forget the message of Hebrews 12:2-3:

> *Keep your eyes on Jesus, who both began and finished this race we're in. Study how He did it. Because He never lost sight of where He was headed—that exhilarating finish in and with God—He could put up with anything along the way: cross, shame, whatever. And now He's there, in the place of honor, right alongside God. When you find yourselves flagging in your faith, go over that story again, item by item, that long litany of hwostility He plowed through. That will shoot adrenaline into your souls* (The Message).

—◊—

Kara persevered. She refused to quit and set realistic goals even when she had setbacks of sore knees and Achilles heel pain. She successfully trained and ran in her first 5K race. Since then she has competed in many more races, even a marathon. She learned that as a Christian as well as runner, she needs to keep up a consistent pace and press toward the goal. The Holy Spirit living within supplies her with all the power and strength to run the race and persevere.

Endnotes

1. W. E. Vine, Vine's *Expository Dictionary of Old and New Testament Words*, (Old Tappan, NJ: Fleming H. Revell Company, 1981), 244.

2. *Runner's World* (August 1991).

3. Dick Innes, "Thank God for Second Chances," (Lifehelp Ministries, Living Message Fellowship, 1999).

4. Anne & Ray Ortlund, *You Don't Have to Quit*, (Nashville, TN: Oliver Nelson, 1986), 25.

5. Sermon Central, http://www.sermoncentral.com/SearchResults30 .asp, (Accessed March 2009).

The Perseverance Test

Personal reflection questions/discussion

1. How are you running with determination and resolution to finish your race? What obstacles are in your way?

2. Do you look for divine opportunities to minister to others and help them also to win the race? How?

3. Are there things that are weighing you down and keeping you from persevering as a leader?

4. What season of ministry/business are you going through right now? How can you persevere?

5. What is the connection between discipline and perseverance?

6. As you look at your life, do you see yourself as one who perseveres or one who gives up too easily. How can you grow in perseverance?

—∿—

Chapter 19

The Success Test

Effective leaders never forget where they came from.

When I was a young pastor, I felt successful since new people were being added to our church nearly every week. Every year our church was growing by 300 new people. It was very exciting. I took our leadership team to conferences and often heard about the hard times many pastors were going through. I remember thinking, "If these pastors would pray more (like us!), I'm sure they would not have all of these problems."

A few years later I woke up to the fact that we *were* having problems, and then I realized how prideful I had been a few years earlier. Obviously prayer is very important, but I had become proud of the way we prayed and felt we really knew what we were doing, and we were doing it better than others! I had faced the "success test" God put before me and failed. Would He allow me to face the test again and pass it?

—※—

We are all driven to succeed in life. Christian success is pleasing God with your life. That's the bottom line. But other things often fuel our efforts to succeed. Frequently we are driven by comparison and competition motives, just like I was when I thought our church leadership was just a little bit better than most because we prayed a lot and didn't seem to have big problems. I had fallen into the comparison trap when I should have compared our success with how it was pleasing God.

Christian success is pleasing God with your life.

C.S. Lewis said it pretty well when he talked about pride and competition.

> Pride gets no pleasure out of having something, only out of having more of it than the next man.... It is the comparison that makes you proud: the pleasure of being above the rest. Once the element of competition has gone, pride has gone. Pride is competitive by its very nature: that is why it goes on and on.[1]

Success can be our greatest test. Why? It can produce pride or the feeling that we have done this on our own.

Success can be our greatest test. Why? It can produce pride or the feeling that we have done this on our own. We no longer see success as simply pleasing God with our lives, but we believe we had the major part in our own success. Moses cautioned the Israelites against this tendency to take the credit for their success. He said they would become proud and forget God:

> For when you have become full and prosperous and have built fine homes to live in, and when your flocks and herds have become very large and your silver and gold

192

have multiplied along with everything else, be careful! Do not become proud at that time and forget the Lord your God, who rescued you from slavery in the land of Egypt (Deuteronomy 8:12-14).

The story of King Uzziah in the Bible tells of a successful, smart, and popular king who ruled well. His kingdom became powerful, but his success went to his head. He started to think that he would do whatever he wanted even if it was not what God wanted. *"But after Uzziah became powerful, his pride led to his downfall..."* (2 Chron. 26:16 NIV). Although he had done many good things to help God's people, he did not give God the credit. When he started doing things his way, God was not pleased. The final straw came when he entered the inner room of the temple. Only the priests were allowed there. God struck him with leprosy and he lived the rest of his days as an outcast.

Another biblical king was also tested with success. Nebuchadnezzar was the mighty king of the Babylonian Empire. He was known for his incredible achievements, but he had no room for God in his kingdom. Late in his reign, Nebuchadnezzar had a wake-up call. Overnight, he went from being a powerful king to a wandering madman. He grew long hair and nails, roaming the hillsides grazing on grass. Seven years into his malady, Nebuchadnezzar returned to his senses. He realized his lifelong mistake of taking the credit for his success. He became a God-fearing man, recognizing that God is a mightier king who rules a Kingdom that lasts forever.

Nehemiah was a prophet in the Bible who passed the success test early. As a leader, Nehemiah resisted pride in his own achievements and gave due credit to God, as well as acknowledging the efforts of others. It's an important lesson for all of us. The God of Heaven will give us success. But it's all about Him. We are God's servants to help Him carry out His plans, His desires, His agenda in order to build His program, not ours.

Thomas Monaghan, the founder of Domino's Pizza, is a modern-day success story. He grew up in foster homes and an orphanage after his father died when he was 4 and his mother decided she could not take care of her two sons. He has no college degree. He founded Domino's Pizza with his brother who later traded his share for a Volkswagen Beetle.

Monaghan says he went through an unfulfilling materialistic phase when he became rich. He bought antique cars, yachts, and the Detroit Tigers baseball team. Then he sold Domino's Pizza in 1998 for $1 billion at age 61. Since getting out of the pizza business, he has focused on philanthropy and his faith. He says he is now invested "in helping people get to heaven." His advice to anyone who will listen is this:

> Wealthy or not, put God first. Pray to God to ask what His will is. Listen and follow. Don't build an empire. Grow a company by serving employees, customers and suppliers. A CEO life of extravagance is nothing more than the sin of pride. Getting rich can be enjoyable. Giving it away—fulfilling![2]

Be Teachable and You Will Grow Successfully

Leaders who are not teachable are spiritually smug. They feel like they are doing just fine and resist God's showing them areas He wants to change in their lives. In Acts 18, Apollos was teaching what he knew—the baptism of John. He was an eloquent speaker and knew the Scriptures. When Aquila and Priscilla took him aside and explained in detail the way of God more accurately, Apollos didn't say, "Can't you see how popular I am? I'm God's man of the hour, and I don't need to learn from you!" Instead, he was teachable and willing to listen. He made the necessary changes in his beliefs and as a result became a great help to the church (see Acts 18:27). John Maxwell, in his book *Leadership Bible*, has this to say about Apollos:

> What impresses me about Apollos is his teachability. He never thought he had learned so much that he couldn't

improve his game. Luke points out several facts about this man: He came from a cultured city (v. 24). He was an educated man (v. 24). He knew the Scriptures well (v. 24). He'd been taught the Christian faith (v. 25). He had an obvious gift (v. 25). He taught truth accurately (v. 25). He taught truth passionately (v. 26).

But the key to Apollos' success in the ministry and the helping to grow the kingdom of God was his teach-ability! Leaders face the danger of contentment with status quo. After all, if a leader already possesses influence and has achieved a level of respect, why should he or she keep growing? Your growth determines who you are. Who you are determines who you attract. Who you attract deter-mines the success of your organization.[3]

How Do You Handle Compliments?

A friend of ours gave us this analogy which helped us. When someone gives you a compliment, you respond "thank you" and receive the compli-ment like a flower handed to you. As you receive each compliment, by the end of the day you have accumulated a bouquet of flowers you offer to God the Father who gave you the ability that led to the compliments being given to you. It keeps everything in perspective.

Be Ready to Fight Spiritual Battles

To pass the success test as a Christian leader, we need to see ourselves as spiritual warriors. A warrior knows in his heart that he will not go anywhere in God without a fight! He is ready to fight the spiritual battles that must be fought to see God's Kingdom advance in the Church, in individual lives, in business, and in the community. Leaders with warrior hearts are those who do not run away in the heat of battle. They can be counted upon to run straight into the battle. *"...He runs at me like a warrior"* (Job 16:14 NKJV). A leader knows that just as Jesus had to pay a price to advance the Kingdom of God, he will pay a price too. A leader's sense of mission enables him to maintain values and principles when confronted with great adversity.

In Matthew 11:12, Jesus says the Kingdom of Heaven is taken hold of by warrior-like people who turn from sin to Christ and continue to resist satan in a fight of faith by the power of the Spirit: *"...the kingdom of heaven has been forcefully advancing, and forceful men lay hold of it"* (NIV). This kind of leader knows that if God has called him, he will succeed and fulfill God's vision, plan, and purpose in the Kingdom of God.

Here is another picture of a leader who passed the success test. Brother Lawrence (whose real name was Nicholas Herman) lived in the 1600s. God taught him to "practice the presence of God" in all he did and said. His success was found solely in fulfilling his call in ministry by accomplishing even those menial tasks with this practice in mind. After his death, his close friend observed that Brother Lawrence desired only God to witness what he did and that his only personal reward was God Himself. Brother Lawrence passed the success test! He is an example for all of us.

—⚍—

I'm glad that I discovered, as a young pastor, that success can easily lead to pride. I started to believe that we were having great success because we prayed so diligently. Although it is certainly important to be a person of prayer, when we shift the focus to ourselves, we fall into pride. We begin to think more highly of ourselves than we ought. At the same time, we begin to think less of others than we should. It's a no-win situation! The best remedy for pride is two bent knees. I learned that the God of Heaven will give us success. But it's all about Him. We are God's servants to help Him carry out His plans, His desires, and His agenda in order to build His program, not ours.

Endnotes

1. Clive Staples Lewis, *The Complete C.S. Lewis Signature Classics*, (HarperCollins, 2002), 90.

2. "Billionaire traded materialism for true happiness," Del Jones interview, *USA Today* (September 19, 2005).

3. John C. Maxwell, Editor, *The Maxwell Leadership Bible* (Nashville, TN: Thomas Nelson, 2003), 1351.

The Success Test

Personal reflection questions/discussion

1. What is the real definition of success in God's eyes?

2. How do we keep success from turning into pride and an inflated ego of confidence in self?

3. How does a teachable spirit help with the success test?

4. How important is it for a leader to "run like a warrior"?

5. What are the spiritual battles you are fighting as a leader? Are you winning?

6. How do we practice the presence of God?

—◊—

Chapter 20

The Timing Test

Effective leaders understand times and seasons.

It seemed evident that God operated on a different timetable than Ashley's. *Why couldn't He hurry up and answer my prayer for my house to sell?* Ashley thought. A university professor on the West Coast, Ashley was trying to sell her house so she could take a new job at a university in Florida. The job offer had come out of the blue, and it was something she had desired for some time. She would be closer to her ailing father, and most of her extended family lived in Florida. It seemed the perfect opportunity, and she felt God's hand was in it. So when she put her house in California up for sale and bought a new house in Florida, she thought it would be smooth sailing. Things seemed to be progressing splendidly. It certainly seemed as though God's timing was in everything that had transpired. She had the whole summer to sell her house.

But the house was not selling. She found people had little interest in it and no offers. It was August 10, and she had to leave the next day to drive cross country with her belongings so she could arrive on time for her teaching position in Florida. She started to have second thoughts. Had she made a complete mistake in understanding God's will in this decision to move east? Maybe she had missed His timing in carrying it out? She could not afford two mortgages. She was in a pinch and needed an answer. "I need help, and I need it now! I must know for sure You are in this move and that You are working in my life," Ashley cried out to God.

—⁓—

"There is a time for everything..." says Ecclesiastes 3:1. A leader will pass the timing test when he understands that he must do the right thing at the right time. Timing really is everything. A business can open prematurely and result in bankruptcy, while another business flourishes because of right timing. An author can write a book that makes the bestseller list, while another book written by the same author can languish on a shelf collecting dust.

The importance of timing is evident throughout the Bible. Abraham had his son Isaac tied up on the altar ready to sacrifice his son following God's command, when a ram, a substitute sacrifice, was caught in a nearby bush. Joseph was sent to Egypt in a series of events that lead to the rescue of his family later. There are multitudes of other illustrations of God's timing events in order to work out for His people. In the New Testament, a man named Ananias in Damascus saw a vision to go to Straight Street and preach to a man named Saul. He wasn't very eager to do this because Saul was the leader of persecutions against the Church, but Saul had had his own encounter with Jesus on the road to Damascus and was ready to receive the message in God's timing.

We can have an idea or a vision and we want to fulfill it immediately, but the timing is not yet right.

A leader knows that he or she must be tuned to the Lord to know His timing for marriage, having children, starting a new job, starting a new church, and building a new business. Many times we can have an idea or a vision and we want to fulfill it immediately, but the timing is not yet right. Moses had the proper vision—deliver the children of Israel from Egypt—but he missed the Lord's timing by 40 years when he killed an Egyptian and ended up in the back side of a desert. The Scriptures tell us that Jesus' enemies tried to kill Him various times but His time "had not yet come."

I know a man who as a child and teenager felt sure that he was called to ministry and that he would someday be a pastor. However the timing wasn't right. He had the passion, the calling, and the heart for God, but he first needed to learn people skills. His paths led him into the hard knocks of building his own business and learning to deal with employees and customers. After many years of honing and preparing, God opened the door and he now is serving his local church as a full-time pastor. Had he jumped straight into ministry as an untested young man, the timing would have been all wrong.

It's a Matter of Time

The Bible is filled with examples of those who went through God's timing tests. Jesus Himself went through His heavenly Father's timing test. He was God's Son, but for His first 30 years He lived with His family and worked in a carpenter's shop, learning the trade of a carpenter. It was hard work, and I'm sure at times monotonous. Even at a young age, He could easily have sat down with the Rabbis and taught them, but God put Him in the carpentry shop to learn to work with His hands and do manual labor. In this training time, Jesus learned to do those things a carpenter does well—repair things and build things from scratch. In the carpentry shop Jesus learned how to sand wood when He needed to, and to polish at other times. He learned how to see the potential in a piece of wood just as He sees the potential in you and me today. When He was ready, in God's timing, Jesus started His public ministry.

Joseph went through a long, lonely timing test starting as a young boy. His grand dreams about how God would use him were misunderstood, and his brothers thought, "This kid must be out to lunch!" You probably know the story. They sold him into slavery, and he ended up in Egypt. In this preparation place, God tested him time and time again because the call of God was so great on his life. If you're going through some hard times right now, rest assured, God probably has greater things than you can ever imagine in store for you in your future. Your test of timing today is helping you grow and develop to become more like Jesus.

In Joseph's experience, even when he did the right thing and avoided his boss' wife's advances, he was thrown into jail anyway. Again he had to experience hard times before they got better. Sometimes you may feel you are doing what God wants you to do, and it gets worse. In jail, Joseph persevered. He heard from God and interpreted the dreams of two prison mates.

But Joseph was forgotten in jail, even though he had accurately interpreted the dreams of the butler and the baker. Finally, in the timing of the Lord, word got out about this dream-interpreter, and he was brought before the king and properly interpreted the dream that was terrifying him. Then Pharaoh pardoned Joseph and made him second in command of the whole empire of Egypt. Through these experiences, Joseph learned to be an obedient child of God, trusting Him for His timing. (See Genesis 37:39–40.)

I heard teacher, Joyce Meyer, say on her television program that "God's timing and how long we have to wait is based on how well we behave while we're waiting." Well said!

Times of Discipline

Genesis 8:22 says that as long as the earth remains there will be seasons. Life is filled with seasons or chapters in which we must discern God's timing. God intervenes in your life purposefully. Nothing is by coincidence or luck. God always has a plan and a purpose for everything He does or allows.

God intervenes in your life purposefully.

We often learn most in tough seasons or times of discipline. Hebrews 12:5-11 explains how God takes us through seasons or times of discipline so we can learn from them:

> *And have you forgotten the encouraging words God spoke to you as His children? He said, "My child, don't make light of the Lord's discipline, and don't give up when He corrects you. For the Lord disciplines those He loves, and He punishes each one He accepts as His child." As you endure this divine discipline, remember that God is treating you as His own children. Who ever heard of a child who is never disciplined by its father? If God doesn't discipline you as He does all of His children, it means that you are illegitimate and are not really His children at all. Since we respected our earthly fathers who disciplined us, shouldn't we submit even more to the discipline of the Father of our spirits, and live forever? For our earthly fathers disciplined us for a few years, doing the best they knew how. But God's discipline is always good for us, so that we might share in His holiness. No discipline is enjoyable while it is happening—it's painful! But afterward there will be a peaceful harvest of right living for those who are trained in this way.*

The Lord disciplines you so that you may share in His holiness. God is preparing you in holiness for His service! It is not always pleasant, and it may seem like everything is going wrong and nothing is happening. But if you allow yourself to be trained during the experiences, they produce a harvest.

Sometimes we try to place the blame for our season of discipline on the devil. Other times we may think that we did something wrong and God is correcting us. But this may not be the case. There are certainly times when we need to resist the devil, but sometimes we give him too much credit.

We may be in God's "hold time" simply because He is preparing us for something that is so good it would blow our minds if we knew all of the details about it today.

Relinquish Your Agenda for God's Timing

Proverbs 16:9 says, *"We can make our plans, but the Lord determines our steps."* Ralph had it all planned out—he would give one year of his life to serve God. He gave notice to his employer, packed his things, and off he went: leaving Germany and its comforts to become a volunteer in Youth With A Mission. He would join a Discipleship Training School in South Africa and travel for a few months. However, God's plan was different. After the first course, all attempts to extend his visa for traveling purposes failed. God's plan was becoming clearer: He had to continue studying to be able to stay in the country. "Miraculously" another course was offered that impacted him so much that he immediately felt the urge to teach what he had just been given. He ended up spending five years in South Africa teaching the Bible. "Looking back," he recalls, "God's ways seemed so different from mine. I am glad that God made me stay, through circumstances I could not control. It was not easy to give up my plans initially, but I am glad I did." Ralph was thrilled that he was able to walk out God's plans and timing, but he had to relinquish his own agenda first.[1]

Relax in the Waiting Room

We all have to wait for God's timing, whether it is His timing to get married, start a business, be healed, find a job, get a promotion, or for our house to sell. God wants us to learn what we have to learn in the waiting room. Sometimes we are eager to get on with life and advance and explore new things, but the Lord holds us back because we are not yet ready to go. In the wait time, He will teach us what we need to know.

God wants us to learn what we have to learn in the waiting room.

During this time in the waiting room we may discover how to approach and discuss a sensitive matter with our spouse. Or God may show us the best way to confront an employee or friend about a matter. We can trust God's timing. God always answers our prayers. Sometimes His answer is not the one we want, but it is always for the best. Keep trusting, and you'll pass the timing test.

———

With a heavy heart, Ashley placed the last of her belongings in the U-Haul and turned to take one last glimpse of her house. It looked as though she would face severe financial hardship—maybe even lose her house in Florida, if this house did not sell. Deep inside she knew that God's seeming lack of activity did not imply a lack of concern on His part. She knew He cared about her and was interested in every aspect of her life. But how long did she have to wait?

After driving all day, Ashley pulled into a hotel for the night. Her phone rang. It was her real estate agent. "A couple just came to see your house and they are very interested," she said. The next day, the agent called again. Another party was interested. They now had not one, but two offers on the house!

"Thank you, Jesus!" Ashley rejoiced. "I guess You do have your own timetable, and as your child, I've inherited Your day planner!

Endnote

1. Ralph Muenstermann, "All Planned Out," *God Stories 2* (Lancaster, PA: Regional Church of Lancaster County, 2007), 276.

The Timing Test

Personal reflection questions/discussion

1. Describe a timing test that you have had. How did you react while you waited?

2. Have you ever gone through a time of divine discipline where you wondered about God's timing?

3. Have you ever had to relinquish your own agenda to discover God's timing? How?

4. What should we do while we are waiting for God's timing?

5. Why is it so much easier to focus on "doing" rather than "waiting"?

—⁓—

Chapter 21

The Kingdom Test

An effective leader focuses on the eternal Kingdom.

A few months ago, Pastor Andrew had gazed out into a congregation where barely a seat remained empty. Not so today. There were large gaps at seats where entire families had sat and worshiped at The Good Shepherd Church, but now they were gone. They had departed to join Lighthouse Fellowship that had just begun a few miles away. Without warning, they had exited the proverbial back door of Good Shepherd.

Andrew had been the pastor of Good Shepherd Church for many years. The church had experienced steady growth and Andrew felt grateful for how his congregation was pursuing Christ's commission to go and make disciples as they reached out to their community. He thought they had been a tight-knit group. So it was disheartening to have the exodus of families that had been a vital part of the congregation.

It was baffling. He had read the "top reasons why people leave your church." He knew that sometimes people yearn for another style of worship or music or a different style of preaching. But he was bewildered. God had been faithful to grow their church and make an impact on their community. People had seemed enthusiastic—until Lighthouse Fellowship appeared on the horizon. OK, maybe they didn't have a snappy new image like Lighthouse Fellowship, but was that any reason for losing so many members?

He tried to console himself, "We probably have 'quality' over 'quantity,'" he thought. He knew he shouldn't feel this way, but it took everything Andrew could muster to keep from resenting the new church. Did he care only about his own church and the impact they made on his city, or would he become a Kingdom-minded pastor and make every effort to work with other churches in his community to see Jesus glorified in their city? Would he pass the Kingdom test?

—⚏—

Some pastors, like Andrew, do not really give too much thought to other churches in their city or region because they are only focused on their own local church. They have not yet learned to be Kingdom pastors. Sometimes it takes a wake-up call, like losing some church members, to test a leader in his Kingdom-mindedness!

What is Kingdom-mindedness? A few years ago a Catholic church in England gave money to finance a youth pastor in a Pentecostal church in their city who needed a youth pastor. The Kingdom of God was more important to them than their own local church. That is Kingdom-mindedness.

Are we building our Kingdom or God's Kingdom?

All of the tests in this book could be wrapped up into the Kingdom test because if we are truly living by the principles of the Kingdom of God, we will be passing the 21 tests of life and leadership discussed in this book. We are instructed in Matthew 6:33 to seek first the Kingdom of

God and all of these things will be added unto us. Rick Warren has said it so well: "It is not about us."[1]

The bottom line is very simple. Are we building our Kingdom or God's Kingdom? God will take us through tests to build our character and make us more able to live in the grace of God and build His Kingdom. We then no longer care who gets the credit, as long as our God is glorified.

The story is told that John Wesley, a founder of Methodism, changed his view about church division after a dream in which he was first transported to the gates of Hell.

He asked, "Are there any Presbyterians here?"

"Yes," was the reply.

"Any Roman Catholics?"

"Yes."

"Any Congregationalists?"

"Yes."

He hesitated, then said, "Not any Methodists, I hope!"

To his dismay the answer was "Yes."

Suddenly in his dream he stood at the gate of Heaven. Once again he asked, "Are there any Presbyterians here?"

"No," was the reply.

"Any Roman Catholics?"

"No."

"Any Congregationalists?"

"No."

Then he asked the question which most interested him: "Are there any Methodists here?"

He was shocked to receive the same stern reply, "No!"

"Well then," he asked in surprise, "please tell me who *is* in Heaven?"

"Christians!" was the jubilant answer. From that dream Wesley determined that unity was essential to the church's success in her mission.[2]

After serving for 15 years as a senior pastor, our mega-church decentralized into eight individual churches and we released each leader and congregation to decide if they wanted to stay with our family of churches or move out on their own. One of our churches in Brazil decided to leave the DOVE family and strike out on their own. It was hard to see them go because we were a family and had so much history together. But we realized that as a Kingdom-minded church we must release them and encourage them as they moved to another arena in the Kingdom. Today the church is flourishing, and we have maintained friendly relationships with the precious people of that church.

It is my belief that faithful churches of many different denominations can work together.

It is my belief that faithful churches of many different denominations can work together, united for the Gospel, reaching a lost world, and building His Kingdom. I just returned a few days ago from the West Coast after spending a few days with a group of pastors and Christian leaders from many denominations who had come together at a retreat center to pray. They were Southern Baptist, American Baptist, Lutheran, Presbyterian, Church of God, Assembly of God, Calvinist, Armenian, Independent, Black, White, Native American...the list went on and on. And they had one goal—to experience God's Kingdom together in their city! They were passing the Kingdom test.

Unity Is God's Desire

Mike is a local youth leader who has seen first hand how Christian leaders can unite and be like-minded in an effort to work together to bring in the harvest. He says:

> When I first started in youth ministry, I was introduced to other youth leaders in the area. They were mostly from different churches, and I didn't know how that would work. Would there be any unity in the group? I quickly discovered, however, that these brothers in the Lord were

210

my most trusted allies. We didn't argue or debate about theologies or philosophy. We prayed together, laughed together, and even cried together. It wasn't about competition, but about joining together to win as many as possible to the Gospel of Jesus Christ. No one was better than the other, but we all had a common goal—to see Jesus move in our hearts and in the hearts of the lost and hurting.

I praise God for allowing me to get to know such a wonderful group of men. I have been truly blessed, and I know that if I had allowed the devil to speak disunity or pride in my heart, I would have missed out on wonderful friendships and ministry. May we all join together to win as many as possible for Jesus. May we stop the gossip and slander in our home churches and our communities. We have much work to do, and if we allow Satan to divide us we will be a dim light in a very dark world. We must repent of the sin of separation and ask God to bring together again His Holy Church. Titus 3:9 admonishes us to *"avoid foolish controversies and genealogies and arguments and quarrels about the law, because these are unprofitable and useless."*[3]

His Kingdom Plan

God has a plan for everyone. Everyone has a job to do in the Kingdom. *"For we are God's masterpiece. He has created us anew in Christ Jesus, so that we can do the good things He planned for us long ago"* (Eph. 2:10). My friend Jerry, a business owner, recently had the opportunity to be involved in setting up a non-profit foundation. In the process, he decided to research other foundations and was inspired by one named The W.K. Kellogg Foundation. The founder W.K. Kellogg is best known as the inventor of corn flakes and founder of the cereal giant. In the early

1900s while other founders of big industry were building summer cottages with 40 car garages, he felt his money was better used in helping people help themselves. In 1934 he set up a foundation that to this day donates millions of dollars a year to helping people in need all over the world.

This is a man who "had it all," but chose to use his wealth to help others. He wanted to do good and did so by channeling money to those in need. So what does God want us to do? The Bible tells us in Ephesians 2:10 that He wants us to do good. In fact, we are His masterpiece, and He created us anew in Jesus so we can do good things.

Jerry, my business friend, understands Kingdom building. He says, "Even though God calls us to do many different things in life, each of us is motivated differently. For me, I love to give. It gives me energy and excitement. For some, it's serving, or teaching—or it could be many other things. We may not have the resources in the large way that Mr. Kellogg did, but God wants us to bless people by doing good the way He called us."[4]

Kingdom Tests

The Bible says that *"the kingdom of God is not a matter of eating and drinking, but of righteousness, peace and joy in the Holy Spirit"* (Rom. 14:17 NIV). God will take us through tests to build our character so that we experience *"righteousness, peace and joy in the Holy Spirit."* The tests we go through may be hard. Abraham Lincoln was a man who overcame incredible setbacks and disappointments in his life before he became president of the United States. His mother died when he was 9 years old, and he grew up poverty-stricken. Abe had less than one year of formal education. As a young man, he lost his job as a store clerk. He later became a partner in a business that failed and left him with a large debt. After courting a young lady for years and asking for her hand in marriage, he was rejected. Later he met a young woman he had an interest in, but she died.

In his early 30s, he decided to run for state office and lost. He ran again and lost. Finally after several years he was elected, but when reelection time came two years later, he lost again. At age 40 he was rejected for another political appointment and suffered a nervous break-down. He also had a son who died during this time. In his mid-forties, he ran for the Senate and was defeated. A few years later, when he ran for the vice-president of the United States, he lost. Finally, at age 51, he was elected president of the United States!

Abe Lincoln refused to quit. He was a godly man who persevered and went on to become one of the greatest presidents of the United States. During the Civil War, he led the nation with wisdom and patience, and is known as the Great Emancipator for helping to abolish slavery in the United States. If this great man had quit in the wilderness, who knows what would have happened to the course of history in the United States. Lincoln faced the tests and persevered to victory.

Hebrews 12:2 gives us great advice for moving ahead when faced with tests. *"Let us fix our eyes on Jesus...who...endured the cross..."* (NIV). Jesus endured the cross, the most horrible pain and suffering imaginable, and yet He persevered.

Leaders must keep their eyes on Jesus, only then can they persevere and enter the "perseverance to victory" season. When leaders enter this season, they have decided to finish the plan God has given them. These are the kinds of leaders God wants to use today. They refuse to give up as they continue to trust Jesus, who is their Source of strength and help, and experience in His Kingdom.

—⁓—

The Good Shepherd Church was confronted by the reality of numeri-cal decline. It was not easy for Pastor Andrew to lose members to another church. He not only had to grapple with the issues of how a church should measure success, he had to be willing to become a Kingdom-minded pastor who could look at the big picture of building up the Body of Christ. He knew his members were growing in faith and discovering, developing, and using their gifts. And he knew that at Lighthouse Fellowship they were doing the same. Together, as churches in their broader community, they could be God's instruments of hope and love to the people Jesus gave His life to rescue. He would *"make every effort to keep the unity of the Spirit through the bond of peace"* (Eph. 4:3 NIV). The Body of Christ included the other churches in their city and other believers around the world. He would do his part in helping God's people develop and use their gifts in service within the Body of Christ and the community and in partnership with other believers around the world—this included praying for and working with Lighthouse Fellowship.

Endnotes

1. Rick Warren, *Purpose Driven Life*, (Grand Rapids, MI: Zondervan Publishing Company, 2002), 1.

2. http://www.sermoncentral.com/SearchResults30.asp (Accessed April 17, 2009).

3. Mike Wenger, "Unity is Awesome," *God Stories from Lancaster County* (Lancaster, PA: The Regional Church of Lancaster County, 2006), 55.

4. Jerry Weaver, "His Plan for Us," *God Stories from Lancaster County* (Lancaster, PA: The Regional Church of Lancaster County, 2006), 169.

The Kingdom Test

Personal reflection questions/discussion

1. How has your thinking been challenged to incorporate the larger, inclusive Kingdom of God within your region of the world?

2. Are you investing any time in working with others in your region, or are you only investing in your own church/business?

3. Why is unity important to God?

4. How can you encourage your friends who are part of another local church to see beyond their doctrine or their theology and pass the Kingdom test as well?

—⚭—

Afterword

I have two final thoughts in closing.

Twenty-one tests of leadership is just the tip of the iceberg. The 21 tests given in this book are only a few of the tests that I have personally had to face. I am convinced these are some of the major tests leaders face. When we are aware of them, we can face these tests, pass these tests, and go on. Even if we fail, when we are faithless, the Lord is faithful. He will give us another chance. He gave Peter another chance, He gave Jonah another chance, and He gives you and me another chance.

But there is one more important truth that we must understand, lest we live our life in introspection rather than receiving and experiencing His grace moment by moment. Ecclesiastes 11:3 tells us: *"If clouds are full of water, they pour rain upon the earth. Whether a tree falls to the south or to the north, in the place where it falls, there will it lie"* (NIV). Beware of too much introspection. Some things that happen in our lives are for a reason. If clouds are full of water, they pour rain upon the earth. It rains because the clouds are filled with water. And many things that happen in our lives are tests to teach us how to live. However, everything that happens to us is not necessarily a test from God, even though He will use these difficult situations in our lives to make us more like Him. Remember, *"All things work together for good to those who love God, to those who are the called according to His purpose"* (Rom. 8:28 NKJV).

In the second part of the same verse, Ecclesiastes tells us that *"whether a tree falls to the south or to the north, in the place where it falls, there will it lie."* Some things in life just happen, and we must be careful not to fall into the trap of trying to figure every little detail out. Sometimes the tree just fell. No reason. It just fell. Sometimes we need to just let the tree lie right where it is and go on! Stop trying to figure everything out! Refuse further introspection and stop asking why. There may not be an answer to that "why" question you are asking.

For those areas of our lives that are tests we need to pass, let's press in to know the Lord better. Let us trust Him and discern the difference between the tests of life and the "trees that just happen to fall." My prayer is that you will experience great grace from the Lord as you pass the tests of life and leadership, as He prepares you to be the leader He has called you to be.

And as you face each test of life, never forget your Heavenly Father's words of affirmation to you: *"You are my beloved son or daughter, and I am pleased with you!"*

—⁂—

Resources from DOVE International

DOVE Leadership and Ministry School

This school provides practical biblical training as well as Holy Spirit empowered impartation and activation. The school has been training leaders for 20 years. Hundreds of graduates are now successfully engaged in the church and marketplace. Participate in nine weekend intensives and complete the entire school at the live campus or via webcast. The school is also available on demand in the new Global Access School. For details visit dcfi.org/training.

Seminars

One day seminars are available on many of the subjects covered in DOVE International books with Larry Kreider and other DOVE International authors and leaders including a one day seminar on *Passing the 21 Tests of Leadership*.

For more details visit:

dcfi.org/resources/seminar

Author Contact

Larry Kreider, International Director
DOVE International
11 Toll Gate Road
Lititz, PA 17543
Tel: 717.627.1996
www.dcfi.org
LarryK@dcfi.org